Financial Markets in the Capitalist Process

Financial Markets in the Capitalist Process

Douglas Vickers

University of Pennsylvania Press
1978

Library of Congress Cataloging in Publication Data

Vickers, Douglas.
Financial markets in the capitalist process.

Includes bibliographical references and index.
1. Saving and investment. 2. Business enterprises—Finance. 3. Finance. I. Title.
HG4539.V53 332.6 77-20308
ISBN 0-8122-7739-2

Printed in the United States of America

Contents

Preface

In this book I have tried to bring into relationship with each other three significant viewpoints from which the contemporary state of financial theory can be evaluated. The preoccupation of the conventional theory with static, timeless, equilibrium analysis has given rise to an orthodoxy that effectively avoids the pressing problems of uncertainty existing in the world. A new realism and hopefully more meaningful decision criteria, both for business firms (on the demand side of the money capital market) and financial investors (on the supply side), follow when assumptions of general equilibrium are replaced by those of disequilibrium, when the treatment of risk by probability reduction methods gives way to a sounder treatment of uncertainty in its Knightian or Keynesian form, and when a firmer respect for historic time replaces the conventional treatment of time as a serially-dated, logical variable. Disequilibrium, uncertainty, and historic time, along with the pervasiveness of the "false trading" associated with them, provide the perspectives from which new light can be focused on financial theory and from which new analytical thought forms can be advanced.

In the received financial theory, risk has been generally interpreted in terms of the variability of outcomes corraled into subjectively assigned probability distributions. But it is here that historic time, disequilibrium, and the uniqueness of decision situations require serious questions to be raised. For if Keynes, for example, had a clear perception of actual states of affairs in the statements that caption this book, vast areas of economic and financial decision making exist in which probability thought forms can not be relied upon at all. A discipline for coming to grips with the problems raised by the newer perspectives exists, however, in the significant work of Professor G. L. S. Shackle. Following the highly productive leads he has proposed, a groundwork is laid in Part III for decision-making under uncertainty when the variables that bear on decisions are understood as "nondistributional variables," and the notion of *probability* is replaced by that of *possibility* and what Shackle has called "potential surprise." The resulting decision framework is applied in the final chapter to both business firms' investment decisions and the selection of financial asset investments.

In Part I, which is devoted largely to a sorting-out of the ideas involved in both the criticism and reconstruction of financial theory, I have examined the decision problems facing the corporate firm on the demand side of the financial markets. The four chapters in Part II present the essential structure and much of the detail of the equilibrium theory of financial asset prices, together with a critical appraisal of the problems that follow from the fact that we do not, contrary to the assumptions of the theory, live in a Walrasian world. The implications of false trading, in both the real and the financial markets of the economy, are explored, and the significance for decision moments of the step-by-step changes in affairs is examined.

Throughout the book I have endeavored to give full acknowledgment to those on whose ideas and published work I have depended. My heaviest intellectual debt is to the work of Professor Shackle, to whom full credit is due for remarkable pioneering and sustained contributions in the areas I have discussed. I shall be happily rewarded if this book is thought to have made a meaningful use of an idea set to which Professor Shackle has proprietary rights. My debt to the architects of the conventional theory from which I dissent will also, I trust, be adequately clear. In Part II the reader will find full acknowledgment of the equilibrium theoretic contributions of Sharpe, Lintner, Mossin, Tobin, Hamada, Haley, Schall, and others, and to the disequilibrium theorists including Clower, Leijonhufvud, Grossman, and Davidson.

A heavy personal debt over a long period has been incurred to Professor Sidney Weintraub, for whose interest and encouragement I record deep appreciation. I have benefitted greatly from extensive discussion of my ideas with Professors Weintraub, Morris Mendelson, and Jamshed Ghandhi. But I cheerfully absolve them each from responsibility for the form in which my work now appears and for the misuse I might have made of their many valuable suggestions.

The initial draft of this work was completed during my tenure at the University of Pennsylvania in 1976 of the Howard Butcher Visiting Professorship of Finance, and I should like to record my gratitude for the courtesies and excellent facilities I enjoyed at that University. Part of the argument contained in Chapter 3 has already appeared in the *Oxford Economic Papers* and I am grateful to the editors of that Journal for permission to publish the material in its present form.

Douglas Vickers

The orthodox theory assumes that we have a knowledge of the future of a kind quite different from that which we actually possess. . . . At any given time facts and expectations were assumed to be given in a definite and calculable form; and risks . . . were supposed to be capable of an exact actuarial computation. The calculus of probability . . . was supposed to be capable of reducing uncertainty to the same calculable status as that of certainty itself.

John Maynard Keynes (*Quarterly Journal of Economics*, February 1937, pp. 222, 212)

Human decisions affecting the future, whether personal or political or economic, cannot depend on strict mathematical expectation, since the basis for making such calculations does not exist.

John Maynard Keynes, (*General Theory of Employment, Interest, and Money*, p. 162-63)

Equilibrium is blither.

John Maynard Keynes (Quoted in G. L. S. Schackle, *Epistemics and Economics*, p. 233)

It is in the transition (toward an "equilibrium position") that we actually have our being.

John Maynard Keynes (*General Theory of Employment, Interest, and Money*, p. 343)

I

Financial Theory in the Scheme of Things

1

Financial Theory and the Crust of Orthodoxy

The contemporary theory of financial markets and the place of capital in the capitalist process are deeply committed to two interdependent sets of assumptions. These are related to the notion of equilibrium, particularly as that comes to expression in a neo-Walrasian theory of generalized market equilibrium; and the idea of probability, or what I shall refer to as probabilistic reduction methods by which uncertainty is reduced to certainty or certainty-equivalents. The first of these sets of assumptions has meant, moreover, that the theory has been cast in a timeless, static mold, and the richness of market behavior and the stance of economic decision-makers in the flow of historic time have been largely unexplored. Equilibrium, probability, and abstraction from historic time have together formed a crust of orthodoxy, and it is necessary to ask whether the real-world relevance of financial theory has not been seriously impaired.

In this proposition the principal thesis emerges. An examination is now required of the ways in which financial theory assumes a markedly different shape and a heightened potential relevance when its assumptions and objectives are regarded in a sharply different light; when the assumption of equilibrium, for example, is replaced by that of disequilibrium and by an explicit consideration of market behavioral reactions; when the assumption of risk or of a probabilistically quantifiable uncertainty variable is replaced by that of residual uncertainty and a nondistributional variable approach to the understanding of it; and when characteristically atemporal analyses, or the preoccupation with "logical time," are replaced by an examination of actual market transactions in calendar or historic time.

For the third leg of this conceptual trilogy, that of a nondistributional variable approach to the handling of uncertainty, a less clear basis of presupposition and potential for communication may exist.

How, in short, can a decision maker come to grips with "the necessity for action and for decision" in situations where "there is no scientific basis on which to form any calculable probability whatever,"[1] not in an objective sense, a subjective sense, or, to refer to a proposed escape from dilemma that has gained adherence in recent times, in a game theoretic sense?[2]

In this last connection a reconsideration is warranted of both uncertainty analysis and its relevance for financial market theory. In particular, some important proposals in the analytically evocative work of Shackle, dealing notably with his "potential surprise" and "ascendancy" functions, deserve careful appraisal.[3] At issue, we shall see, is the received tradition in the theory of money capital or financial market equilibration, and the relevance of that for decision criteria in the real-world firms that demand and use money capital funds.

In his excellent work on the neoclassical *Theory of Financial Markets,* Jan Mossin has crystallized the issue as to

> what the theory of decision making under uncertainty is all about. . . . The theory deals with *choices among probability distributions.* By choosing one action, we get one probability distribution; by choosing another, we get another. Thus, to make a decision under uncertainty consists in a choice of a probability distribution. When formulated in this way, the nature of the theory becomes clearer.[4]

But unfortunately, the construction of the theory on such presuppositions as these avoids completely the important conception of uncertainty, as distinct from reducible risk, emphasized by Knight,[5] Keynes,[6] and Shackle.[7] By Mossin's own warning, moreover, "the representation of preferences among probability distributions by means of a utility function of wealth is meant to apply to cases of timeless

[1]John Maynard Keynes, "The General Theory of Employment," *Quarterly Journal of Economics* (February 1937): 214.

[2]Cf. G. L. S. Shackle, *Epistemics & Economics* (Cambridge: Cambridge Univ. Press, 1972), p. 161, and pp. 422ff for a discussion of "Game Theory's Exclusion of Tactical Surprise," and the same author's *Decision, Order and Time in Human Affairs* (Cambridge: Cambridge Univ. Press, 1969), pp. 98, 100.

[3]Cf. the perceptive review article by Alan Coddington, "Creaking Semaphores and Beyond: A Consideration of Shackle's 'Epistemics and Economics,'" *Philosophy of Science* 26 (1975); and E. Roy Weintraub, "'Uncertainty' and the Keynesian Revolution," *History of Political Economy* (1975): 531, who says of Shackle that "in a large number of books, monographs, and articles he has presented this view and its ramifications to deaf-eared economists."

[4]Jan Mossin, *Theory of Financial Markets* (Englewood Cliffs, N.J.: Prentice-Hall, 1973), p. 6, italics in original.

[5]Frank H. Knight, *Risk, Uncertainty and Profit* (Boston: Houghton Mifflin, 1921) London School of Economics reprint No. 16, 1948, p. 19.

[6]See "General Theory of Employment."

[7]See *Epistemics & Economics.*

prospects."[8] And Mossin recognizes that the crux of the matter is that "in the real world *temporal* prospects, not timeless ones, are the rule rather than the exception."[9] An appropriate accounting for time, for "historic" as distinct from "logical" time, will render suspect not only the utility analysis to which Mossin has referred, but also the core of the treatment of uncertainty itself.[10]

It will be necessary to ask whether what Hicks has called "the pure theory of portfolio selection," or what I shall refer to as the neo-Walrasian equilibrium theory of financial asset pricing, does in fact offer a solid foundation for decision making by financial investors and by real-world firms. Hicks has noted the theory's underlying assumption of "perfect markets" and "perfect competition." He acknowledges that "such a theory will not often apply to investment in real capital . . . ," and that "it is by no means universally applicable to Stock Exchange and other financial investment."[11] But when he goes on to argue that alternative hypotheses, such as that of Shackle, for example, "come under suspicion at once because of their apparent inapplicability to portfolio theory," we are entitled to question whether the fault might not lie in the fact that the existing norms of the portfolio theory itself are not adequately and securely grounded.[12]

Scope and Objectives of Financial Market Theory

False Trading in the Real and the Financial Markets

My critique of conventional financial theory will be concerned with the question of market equilibration. This has to be viewed against the background of the equilibrating assumptions of the more usual general equilibrium theory. This involves the assumption of Walrasian tatonnement equilibrating processes and the generally accompanying postulate of Edgeworthian recontracting in tentative market confrontations. Implied also is the assumption of infinite market price adjustment velocities in disequilibrium or non-market-clearing situations.

[8]Mossin, *Theory of Financial Markets*, p. 32. We shall bring the utility function analysis into full perspective in a later chapter.

[9]Ibid., italics in original.

[10]Paul Davidson, in his balanced review of Mossin's book in the *Economic Journal* (September 1973): 915, has perceived the nature of the grounds on which financial market theory is now in need of reconstruction. "For most problems in financial theory" he acknowledges, "irreversible time and uncertainty is the essence of the matter," and he laments the "faith in neoclassical parables," which apparently insists on maintaining to the contrary.

[11]John Hicks, *Critical Essays in Monetary Theory* (Oxford: Clarendon Press, 1967), p. 103.

[12]Ibid.

The same equilibrating processes are involved in financial market theory, and this means that important implications of the conventional argument spill over from the real market theory, where the general equilibrium analysis first came to maturity, to the theory of financial markets. In market equilibrating behavior, it is assumed, no transactions are consummated at non-equilibrium prices. In the words of Hicks and of certain of the more recent disequilibrium theorists such as Clower, Leijonhufvud, Grossman, Minsky, and Chick, no "false trading" occurs.[13] Hicks recognized the false trading problem very early. But for practical purposes, and therefore for his ongoing analysis, he assumed it away. Thus,

> in the general case, gains and losses due to false trading only give rise to income effects—effects, that is, which are the same in kind as the income effects which may have to be considered even when we suppose equilibrium prices to be fixed straight away. We have seen again and again that a certain degree of indeterminateness is nearly always imparted by income effects to the laws of economic theory. All that happens as a result of false trading is that this indeterminateness is somewhat intensified. . . . But I think we may reasonably suppose that the transactions which take place at "very false" prices are limited in volume.[14]

But Hicks' dismissal of the problem in this fashion clearly will not do. As Clower has rejoined,

> It is heartening to know that income effects can be ignored if they are sufficiently unimportant to be neglected; but this is hardly a solution to the problem at issue. The essential question is whether the supply and demand functions of traditional analysis are in any way relevant to the formation of market prices in situations where disequilibrium transactions *cannot* be ignored.[15]

The Hicksian false trading assumption is ensconced also in the analysis of financial asset and money capital markets. Fama and Mil-

[13]Robert Clower, "The Keynesian Counter-revolution: A Theoretical Appraisal" in F. H. Hahn and F. P. R. Brechling, eds., *The Theory of Interest Rates* (London: Macmillan, 1965); Axel Leijonhufvud, "Keynes and the Keynesians: A Suggested Interpretation," *American Economic Review* 57 (1967), and the same author's *On Keynesian Economics and the Economics of Keynes* (New York: Oxford Univ. Press, 1968). (See also Robert Clower and Axel Leijonhufvud, "The Coordination of Economic Activities: A Keynesian Perspective," *American Economic Review* 65 [1975]); Herschel I. Grossman, "Theories of Markets without Recontracting," *Journal of Economic Theory* 1 (1969); Hyman P. Minsky, "An 'Economics of Keynes' Perspective on Money," in Sidney Weintraub, ed., *Modern Economic Thought* (Philadelphia: Univ. of Pennsylvania Press, 1977); Victoria Chick, "The Nature of the Keynesian Revolution: A Reassessment," forthcoming in *Australian Economic Papers.*

[14]John R. Hicks, *Value and Capital* (Oxford: Clarendon Press, 1946), p. 129.

[15]Clower, "The Keynesian Counterrevolution," p. 113, italics in original.

ler, for example, in an articulate codification of the theory, have embedded their financial market equilibration in the assumption that

> prices and decisions are tentative; it is agreed that no decisions are executed until an equilibrium set of prices, that is, a set of prices at which all markets can clear, has been determined. Our treatment of this model concentrates on the nature of equilibrium in the capital market; that is, we take equilibrium in the markets for labor and consumption goods as given.[16]

Contrary to this Fama-Miller postulate, however, the argument that market transactions are consummated at non-equilibrium prices constitutes a major thesis in this book. In actual markets, decision makers stand at identifiable points in historic or calendar time and are confronted, as Keynes has observed, with "the necessity for action and for decision." In the actual state of affairs, market transactions are consummated sequentially; there is no Edgeworthian recontracting; decision makers do not live in a Walrasian world in which an omnicompetent auctioneer exists to help things along; and false trading is pervasive. There is need to ask, therefore, how lines of interconnection can be established between the real markets and the financial markets of the economy when the former exhibit demonstrably disequilibrium, as opposed to equilibrium, structures.[17]

If, in actual fact, false trading occurs pervasively in both the real markets and the financial markets of the economy, account will have to be taken of "spillover effects," "redistribution effects," wealth effects, and induced variations in financial market transactors' asset value endowments, all potentially affecting the possibility, uniqueness, and stability of attainable equilibria in the financial markets.[18] It will be salutary, therefore, to look briefly at the implications of this for what has been referred to as the "efficiency" of the money capital or the financial asset market. I shall refer in particular to "information efficiency," which can be taken to imply that "present security prices are costlessly known to all participants and information about future security prices is 'fully reflected' in these present prices."[19]

Financial markets, it is being proposed in this last statement, are "efficient" in the sense that information coming to them from the

[16]Eugene F. Fama and Merton H. Miller, *The Theory of Finance* (New York: Holt, Rinehart and Winston, 1972), pp. 277-78.

[17]Cf. Douglas Vickers, "Finance and False Trading in Nontatonnement Markets," *Australian Economic Papers* (December 1975), and "Disequilibrium Structures and Financing Decisions in the Firm," *Journal of Business Finance and Accounting*, 1, no. 3 (1974).

[18]On "redistribution effects," cf. Grossman, "Theories of Markets without Recontracting," pp. 476f.

[19]Mark Rubenstein, "Securities Market Efficiency in an Arrow-Debreu Economy," *American Economic Review* 65 (December 1975): 812.

underlying real markets of the economy is immediately and efficiently disseminated and assimilated. The situation is akin to that inherent in the knowledge postulates of the neoclassical Walrasian equilibrating parable. Mossin, for example, has drawn the analogy between the activities of the Walrasian auctioneer or the "market manager" and that of security market operators by arguing that "floor trading in actual security markets closely resembles this process, and because of the unusually rapid flow of information, security markets are probably more effective than any other market in eliminating discrepancies between demand and supply."[20] That, of course, may be so. But if it is imagined that the point principally or solely at issue relates to the "efficiency" of the securities markets in assimilating information coming to them, then analysis has already been shunted into a blind alley and a logical dead end. For a larger question relates to the quality, the ease of availability, and the speed and efficiency of dissemination of information in the real markets that lie behind the financial markets; and to the nature of the information itself that emanates from goods markets, labor markets, and real asset markets for onward transmission to the financial markets. For if, in some sense, the information generated in the real markets is "disequilibrium" rather than "equilibrium" information, then the efficiency postulate of the received financial market theory is simply claiming that the latter markets are highly efficient in assimilating false and conceivably misleading information and signals.

On the other hand, in the explanation of investor behavior variations in preferences, expectations, uncertainties, investment opportunities, and what Keynes referred to as "the state of confidence" and "the news" point analysis in the direction not of specifying the *conditions* that could be understood to obtain if the world were *in* a posture of equilibrium, but of the nature and motivation and effects of the *changes* that continually occur in the flow of historic time in which economic decisions are made.[21] This lay behind the *shifting* equilibrium which Keynes had in view. It was necessary, he argued, "not to overlook the fact that it is in the transition that we actually have our being."[22]

The *uniqueness* of decision events in real-world corporate firms (which will be seen in due course to bear upon the inadmissibility of probability thought forms in the description and analysis of such deci-

[20]Mossin, *Theory of Financial Markets*, p. 65.

[21]John Maynard Keynes, *The General Theory of Employment, Interest and Money* (New York: Harcourt, Brace, 1936), pp. 148 and 155.

[22]Ibid., p. 343. Cf. J. A. Kregel, "Economic Methodology in the Face of Uncertainty: The Modeling Methods of Keynes and the Post Keynesians," *Economic Journal* 86 (June 1976).

sion events), and the variability of the *timing* of the confrontation between corporate demanders of money capital funds on the one hand and the financial markets on the other bear on this Keynesian point.

If, moreover, it *is* possible to specify an equilibrium theoretic system and exhibit the conditions that would, by analytic necessity, be satisfied and be shown to hold when a generalized equilibrium obtained, the very achievement of an analytic result of this kind would open the way to a further pressing and important logical problem. In what sense, it would have to be asked, could the *equilibrium conditions* generated by an equilibrium theoretic model be legitimately taken as describing *decision criteria* in demonstrably real world *disequilibrium* situations? Inadequate care has often been taken in relation to this significant logical, or epistemological, problem, and considerations cognate with it will be taken up further.

The Capitalist Process

My title has conjoined the "theory of financial markets" and "the capitalist process." This implies that I am concerned with the determinants of the supplies of, and the demands for, money and financial assets, which occasion the observable state of the financial markets at a specifiable point in time; and with the manner in which both the supplies of, and the demands for, financial assets are dependent on developments, prospects, evaluations, and trends in the underlying real markets of the economy. Financial market developments react back also on real market conditions. I am concerned, in short, with the theory of an actual money-using and mixed capitalist economy, and with its historical, evolutionary, and institutional characteristics.

Account must be taken also of the fact that the financial markets are characterized by extensive speculation. Consider the demand for money, for example, or the Keynesian conception of the *state* (not simply the shape of a given, stable, and smoothly downward sloping function) of liquidity preference. The recognition of the continued presence of speculation in the market provides the linkage between the market for liquidity and the general analysis of uncertainty. Keynes himself, in his interpretation of the demand for money as a store of wealth, wondered why "anyone outside a lunatic asylum would wish to use money" for that purpose, were it not for the fact that the doing of it is "a barometer of the degree of our distrust of our own calculations and conventions concerning the future."[23] Speculation

[23]Keynes, "The General Theory of Employment," p. 216.

against our own lack of knowledge, precipitating a demand for liquidity as "a *substitute* for knowledge," comes clearly into view.[24]

The conjunction of "the financial markets" and "the capitalist process" alerts us also to the fact that vital linkages exist between the prices of financial assets on the one hand and the values of real capital assets on the other. It is the relation between the prices of *financial* assets, implying a specifiable cost of money capital for real-world firms, and the projected income earning ability of *real* capital assets that determines the amount of real capital formation that occurs in the corporate sector of the economy.

The volume of real investment, the sustaining characteristic of the capitalist process itself, turns on the capitalized values of the income streams that real assets can be expected to generate, or on the time vector of the Keynesian "prospective yields" on investments.[25] But these yields are themselves uncertain, and I shall accordingly suggest a method by which the uncertainties involved can be taken adequately into account.

Second, the success or otherwise of entrepreneurial action and of capital formation in the real sector influences the wealth endowments, the variations in them, and the states of confidence or the bullishness-bearishness conjunctures that determine the supply conditions in the money capital or financial asset markets, as well as the demand conditions that exist there.[26]

Third, the relations between the financial markets and the capitalist process also explain the *structures* of both the supplies of and the demands for financial assets or corporate securities. This part of financial market analysis is still insecure, though it is at this point that the new theories of portfolio selection come into relevance, with their

[24]G. L. S. Shackle, *Epistemics & Economics*, p. 216, italics in original. This important matter is not only subtle in its analytical implications but also contains scope for serious misunderstanding. This follows, for example, from the frequent misreading of the seminal work on liquidity demand by James Tobin. In his important "Liquidity Preference as Behavior towards Risk" in the *Review of Economic Studies* 26 (February 1958), Tobin makes it clear that the subject at issue is risk as quantifiable by subjectively assigned probability distributions and not uncertainty in our residual or Keynesian sense at all. What Tobin is concerned with is a theory of liquidity preference which "takes as given the choices determining how much wealth is to be invested in monetary assets and concerns itself with the allocation of these amounts among cash and alternative monetary assets." The argument, in other words, takes no account at all of the uncertainties that generate a genuinely speculative demand for liquidity, and therefore of the influences bearing on the pricing of financial assets that emanate from this critically important source. See also Tobin's "The Theory of Portfolio Selection" in F. H. Hahn and F. P. R. Brechling, eds., *The Theory of Interest Rates* (London: Macmillan, 1965).

[25]J. M. Keynes, *General Theory*, pp. 135 ff.

[26]Cf. Paul Davidson, *Money and the Real World* (London: Macmillan, 1972), chapter 4 for a valuable discussion of "The Demand and Supply of Capital Goods."

homogenization of investment opportunities by a methodologically uniform specification of risks and the determination of a uniquely specifiable, equilibrium, "market price of risk."[27] This line of analysis has focused attention on a conceptualized utility function optimization process in which corporate firms and their capital securities have lost their uniqueness by having their identities submerged in uniformly measurable risks and probable returns. This analysis of the supply side of the money capital market, or of the demand for financial assets, thereby becomes, in effect, what Mossin has referred to as "choices among probability distributions."

Fourth, significant imperfections may exist in the financial markets, and cognizance should be taken not only of the concentration of funds and quasi-monopolistic situations in the supply of money capital, but also of quasi-monopsonistic positions enjoyed by some demanders of funds or suppliers of corporate capital securities. Not all the debt securities of all corporations are saleable in open security markets, for example. So-called "private placements" occur, loans are privately negotiated, wide varieties of "restrictive covenants" are attached to corporate securities of different kinds issued by firms in different economic and management situations, and issue and transactions costs may vary significantly for securities of different kinds and different amounts.[28]

All these considerations imply that financial market theory must explain the yields available on capital securities of different kinds, or, to look at the same matter from the opposite side of the market, the "cost of capital" to the corporate demanders of money capital funds. Here, in effect, the theory must necessarily examine three things: first, the cost of corporate debt capital as compared with common stock or equity capital;[29] second, the determinants of the optimum debt-to-

[27]Cf. Tobin, "Theory of Portfolio Selection"; Harry M. Markowitz, *Portfolio Selection* (New York: Wiley, 1959); Mossin, *Theory of Financial Markets;* Fama and Miller, *Theory of Finance;* Michael C. Jensen, ed., *Studies in the Theory of Capital Markets* (New York: Praeger, 1972), and G. P. Szegö and Karl Shell, *Mathematical Methods in Investment and Finance* (Amsterdam: North-Holland, 1972).

[28]Cf. Douglas Vickers, *The Theory of the Firm: Production, Capital, and Finance* (New York: McGraw-Hill, 1972), p. 110. Axel Leijonhufvud perceptively observes that "it would be incongruous, of course, to combine the 'imperfect' markets for current output and factor services with so-called 'perfect capital markets' in the same model. 'Perfect capital markets' presumes generally shared, certainty-equivalent expectations" *On Keynesian Economics,* p. 57.

[29]The vast literature on this subject, much of which will be engaged in later chapters, has stemmed from the seminal papers of F. Modigliani and M. H. Miller, "The Cost of Capital, Corporation Finance and the Theory of Investment," *American Economic Review* 48 (June 1958), and W. F. Sharpe, "Capital Asset Prices: A Theory of Market Equilibrium under Condition of Risk," *Journal of Finance,* 19 (September 1964): 425-42. See also W. Sharpe, *Portfolio Theory and Capital Markets* (New York: McGraw-Hill, 1970).

equity financing ratios, or the theory of optimum capital structures in corporate firms;[30] and third, the manner in which the debt-equity financing structures in the corporate sector may affect the robustness or "fragility" of the financial system as the economy moves through a possibly financially induced alternation of prosperity and recession and its stages of development and growth.[31]

The work of Jan Mossin has crystallized the conventional theory and draws many of the issues together:

> Market values are determined by the demands of all investors, and this leads us to study the theory of *general equilibrium* in competitive security markets. Without such a model we are unable to foresee the effects of corporate investment and financing decisions. But once we have a theory of share valuation, we also have in hand a theory of optimal financing and investment decisions.[32]

It is precisely the efficiency and relevance of this supposedly inevitable general equilibrium theoretic analysis that I shall call in question in what follows.

Equilibrium Theory

The retreat of economic thought from the stage to which Keynes had brought it, and its devolution into a neo-Walrasian, neoclassical mold, is highly relevant to the tasks in view.

The commitment of financial theory to the thought forms of general equilibrium analysis has been definitive. In their impressive and influential *Mathematical Methods in Investment and Finance*, Szegö and Shell take it for granted that the legitimate maturation of financial analysis must be determined by "a general equilibrium theory," and progress in finance is applauded to the extent that "more and more 'general equilibrium' considerations have been brought to bear on the

[30]A recent development of the theory in this direction, in the spirit of the Modigliani-Miller capital structure irrelevance theorems, can be inspected in Vernon L. Smith, "Corporate Financial Theory under Uncertainty," *Quarterly Journal of Economics* 84 (August 1970), which draws attention to the possibility of "default risk" on corporate bonds; and, "in the context of a general equilibrium model," Joseph E. Stiglitz, "On the Irrelevance of Corporate Financial Policy," *American Economic Review* 64 (December 1974): 855-56, discusses the possible "limitations" imposed on the irrelevance of corporate financial policy by "(1) expectations of real returns dependent on firm financial policy; (2) individual borrowing not a perfect substitute for firm borrowing; (3) bankruptcy."

[31]The concept of "systemic fragility" is due to Hyman P. Minsky. See his "The Modeling of Financial Instability" in *Proceedings of the Fifth Annual Pittsburgh Conference on Modeling and Simulation, 1974*, and his *John Maynard Keynes* (New York: Columbia Univ. Press, 1975).

[32]Mossin, *Theory of Financial Markets*, pp. 1-2, italics in original.

theory."[33] The work of Sharpe, Mossin, Fama, Miller, Jensen, Smith, and Stiglitz is also firmly and confessedly concerned with variations on the equilibrium theme. At the textbook level, the most effective and thorough exploration of the terrain is the work of Haley and Schall, and applications of the general equilibrium asset model to the financial theory of the firm have been made by Bierman and Hass.[34]

The development and generalization of the Walrasian theory has recently been accorded a quasi-definitive formulation by Arrow and Hahn, whose work evinces the respect in which the general equilibrium analysis has diverted macroeconomic thought since Keynes' *General Theory* reconstructed that field.[35] But the acknowledged unfinished agenda of Arrow and Hahn, and their return at the end to the very questions Keynes had tackled, means that the backwardness of the general equilibrium advance should now be apparent. The story of the "irony of Hicks' transmogrification of Keynes' analysis" is by now well known if not yet fully appreciated.[36] Hicks' "Mr. Keynes and the 'Classics'" should now be read in the light of his more recent exploration, if not recantation, in his *The Crisis in Keynesian Economics*, but, together with his neo-Walrasian *Value and Capital*, it did establish an interpretive macroeconomic framework from the shackles of which the theory has not yet unambiguously escaped.[37]

The meaning of the "Keynesian Perplex" and the question of what is the "correct" interpretation of Keynes, or what Keynes said or what he really meant, is relevant to my theme insofar as it bears on three points: first, the necessity of adopting a focus on the nature of the movement and change in the system rather than on describable, if not achievable, equilibrium postures; second, the status of uncertainty and its possible description by quantifiable probability; and third, the extent to which microanalytic foundations provide an underpinning of the macrotheoretical structures.[38]

For the theory of the firm, meshed as it is in the general theory of

[33] Szegö and Shell, *Mathematical Methods*, pp. v, vii.

[34] Charles W. Haley and Lawrence D. Schall, *The Theory of Financial Decisions* (New York: McGraw-Hill, 1973); Harold Bierman, Jr. and Jerome E. Hass, *An Introduction to Managerial Finance* (New York: Norton, 1973), chapter 14.

[35] Kenneth J. Arrow and F. H. Hahn, *General Competitive Analysis* (San Francisco: Holden-Day, 1971). See also James Quirk and Rubin Saposnik, *Introduction to General Equilibrium Theory and Welfare Economics* (New York: McGraw-Hill, 1968) and Robert E. Kuenne, *The Theory of General Economic Equilibrium* (Princeton: Princeton Univ. Press, 1963).

[36] Robert Clower, "Reflections on the Keynesian Perplex," *Zeitschrift für Nationalökonomie* 35 (1975), p. 7.

[37] John R. Hicks, *Econometrica* 5 (April 1937), reprinted in Hicks, *Critical Essays*, pp. 126ff; John R. Hicks, *The Crisis in Keynesian Economics* (Oxford: Clarendon Press, 1974); Hicks, *Value and Capital*.

[38] Clower, "Keynesian Perplex."

value and of optimum economic behavior, the devolution of thought into a timeless, static, equilibrium mold meant that in partaking of the generalized development of the neo-Walrasian orthodoxy, it left behind a potentially richer Marshallian tradition. For Walras, the world at a point in time is exhaustively describable by a system of simultaneous equations in which the economic endowments, factor supplies, knowledge, preferences, and tastes of economic decision makers and optimizers are given. But what has not been accomplished is the transmutation of the theory in such a way as to take account of time and uncertainty and to bring the argument closer to the conditions of real-world markets and thereby to the questions of financial theory. The existing attempts at this transmutation have not been signally successful, and for general equilibrium theory the intertemporal and uncertainty problems have been resolved substantially by defining or assuming them away.

That time must somehow be involved in the analytical scheme of things was acknowledged by Walras himself. In his production model, for example, as distinct from his pure exchange model, it was necessary to begin with fixed or specified factor endowments rather than endowments of finished commodities, and to specify the technological coefficients of production pointing toward profit-maximizing possibilities. It was possible then, it was supposed, to compare the derived demands for inputs and the demands for final outputs at varying tentative prices with available or postulated supplies of each, and to "grope" in some tatonnement fashion to equilibrium price and quantity vectors. It should be noted immediately that as in the Walrasian exchange model there is no false trading, so in the production model there is no false production.[39] But the problem that inhered in the production model was the problem of time.

Consider Walras' specification of the models:

> In *exchange,* (the total existing quantities of) commodities do not undergo any change. When a price is cried, and the effective demand and offer corresponding to this price are not equal, another price is cried for which there is another corresponding effective demand and offer. In *production,* productive services are transformed into products. After certain prices for services have been cried and *certain quantities of products have been manufactured,* if these prices and quantities are not the equilibrium prices

[39]Cf. the very interesting discussion in Chick, "Nature of Keynesian Revolution," of the extent to which Robert Clower's discussion in his "Keynesian Counterrevolution" may have misunderstood and misspecified the relation between the Keynesian and the Walrasian perspectives on these points.

and quantities, it will be necessary not only to cry new prices *but also to manufacture revised quantities of products.*[40]

Clearly, in the italicized clauses the realization of a process and a lapse of time are threatening to emerge. "Production," Walras acknowledges, "requires a certain lapse of time." But the "complication" is immediately assumed away:

> We shall resolve the . . . difficulty purely and simply by ignoring the time element at this point. And later on . . . we shall bring in *circulating capital* and *money* and thereby make it possible for productive services to be transformed into products instantaneously, provided that the consumers pay the interest charges on the capital required for this sort of transformation.[41]

We are pointed here toward the consistent use of the tatonnement process in all of the three Walrasian models: those of pure exchange, pure production, and production with varying degrees of capital intensity.

In relation to the neo-Walrasian extensions from the position Walras himself had reached, Kregel has concluded that "the orthodox approach . . . has not yet succeeded in relaxing its taming assumption concerning perfect foresight and uncertainty."[42] And E. Roy Weintraub has referred to "the inability of the Walrasian system to deal with uncertainty problems."[43] Attempts at resolving this issue have succeeded only in taking the argument further in the direction of "intellectual experiments" and away from real world description and explanation.[44] Of course it may be claimed, as in F. H. Hahn's defense of the theory and his review of Kornai, that "the most obvious explanation of why one studies this theory [general equilibrium], which is known to conflict with the facts, is that one is not engaged in description at all."[45] But that is beside the point. We can acknowledge the elegance of the theory and still call in question the wisdom and efficiency of the wholesale capitulation to it that financial theory in particular has made.

Financial theory, therefore, should now be interested in different questions and different objectives than have been the province of general equilibrium theory. But because that is so, it is analytically

[40]Léon Walras, *Elements of Pure Economics*, trans. William Jaffe, (Homewood, Ill.: Richard D. Irwin, for the American Economic Association, [1926] 1953), p. 242, our italics.

[41]Ibid., p. 242, italics in original.

[42]Kregel, "Economic Methodology," 223.

[43]E. Roy Weintraub, "'Uncertainty' and Keynesian Revolution," p. 545.

[44]Cf. János Kornai, *Anti-Equilibrium* (Amsterdam: North-Holland, 1971), p. 11.

[45]F. H. Hahn, "The Winter of our Discontent," *Economica* (August 1973): 323.

improper to see financial theory persisting in addressing itself to *its* problems by the use of a methodology designed to handle its own and quite different problems. Hahn has conceded as much by acknowledging that "GE is strong on equilibrium and *very weak on how it comes about.* It is a fair generalization to say that the theory has proved so far less helpful in studying *processes* whether of decisions or of information or of organizations."[46]

In concluding his seminal work on the theory of value, Debreu addressed the case in which the character of the consumption and production sets and the resource availabilities in the economy were determinable by uncertain events.[47] From these foundations a theory of "time-state preference" has developed in which (usually complete) markets are understood to exist for claims on future dated commodities whose availability is contingent on the occurrence of specifiable future states or events. In applying the theory to the area of finance and financial markets, Hirshleifer's work has summarized and expounded the principles most thoroughly.[48] But the bridge from the theory to the actual world is unable to bear the weight which the implication of multiple markets has placed upon it. As Malinvaud, a foremost student of the art, has observed,

> We know that neoclassical general equilibrium theory may be applied to an economy for which time and uncertainties must be considered. . . . The markets for future commodities and for contingent commodities, which play an important role in the theory, provide a remote idealization of the observable organization of resource allocation. The reason for the absence of such markets may be that they would not provide an efficient arrangement in practice. While formally appropriate for sustaining an equilibrium, the ideal market system would be too costly to implement. Moreover it might not work properly out of equilibrium: in the separate operation of the various markets no account could be taken of what may be *a priori* known about the particular features of the equilibrium price system, the process for the iterative determination of prices might then be unstable, or too slow, or convergent towards a limit having undesirable properties.[49]

Hirschleifer's method of resolving the case has dealt with "choice over dates and states" when "complete markets for time-state claims"

[46]Ibid., p. 327, my italics.

[47]Gerard Debreu, *Theory of Value, An Axiomatic Analysis of Economic Equilibrium* (New York: Wiley 1959), chapter 7.

[48]J. Hirschleifer, *Investment, Interest and Capital* (Englewood Cliffs: Prentice-Hall, 1970). Cf. also Bernt P. Stigum, "Competitive Equilibrium under Uncertainty," *Quarterly Journal of Economics,* 83 (November 1969), and K. J. Arrow, "The Role of Securities in the Optimal Allocation of Risk-bearing," *Review of Economic Studies* 31 (January 1964).

[49]E. Malinvaud, "Markets for an Exchange Economy with Individual Risks," *Econometrica* 41 (May 1973), pp. 383-84.

can be understood to exist.[50] A system of markets is said to be "complete" when every contingency at every conceivable future time date corresponds to a distinct marketable commodity, in this case a capital security or financial asset. A world in which markets for some conceivable time-state claims or for some objects of choice do not exist is said to be characterized by "incomplete markets." What is involved is the determination of the effective or equilibrium prices in the markets for uncertain or risky claims. And this in turn involves the assumption that "each individual attaches subjective probability estimates . . . to the . . . available time-state sequences," and "risk classes" of securities are imagined to exist as a result.

We should note the less optimistic conclusion that Hirshleifer reaches at the close of his rigorous unfolding of the general equilibrium theoretic approach to financial theory:

> The standard assumption has been that markets are both complete and perfect, so that equilibrium is instantaneously and costlessly attained. . . . But we know that markets do not operate costlessly. . . . Under the time-state model . . . markets cannot really be complete—while under the mean, standard-deviation model . . . they cannot be perfect. The assumption of costless exchange prevents a satisfactory treatment of the debt-equity mix in corporate finance (telling us that it makes no difference!), and leaves no real basis for the existence of money. Finally, a more satisfactory model of the exchange process would perhaps enable a treatment of the *consequences of transactions executed at nonclearing prices,* thus making possible a better connection between the theory of choice and . . . macroeconomics.[51]

But the sway of the general equilibrium theoretic approach to financial theory continues, notwithstanding its failure to produce "integrated model(s) of production in the presence of capital asset market equilibrium" in which "we need know only equilibrium market values."[52] We can doubt, moreover, the efficiency of the further exploration of the generalized market equilibrium conditions in the handling of "incomplete" rather than "complete" markets.[53]

What financial theory needs now to be concerned with is not the "intellectual experiments" involved in unraveling the conditions that could be understood to be satisfied if, on the basis of specifiable assumptions, conditions of "equilibrium" in some definable sense ac-

[50]Hirschleifer, *Investment, Interest and Capital,* chapter 9 *passim.*

[51]Ibid., p. 312, my italics, parentheses in original.

[52]Hayne E. Leland, "Production Theory and the Stock Market," *Bell Journal of Economics and Management Science* 5 (Spring 1974), p. 125.

[53]Steiner Ekern and Robert Wilson, "On the Theory of the Firm in an Economy with Incomplete Markets," *Bell Journal of Economics and Management Science* 5 (Spring 1974): 171.

tually obtained in suitably defined markets. To assume that equilibrium conditions are satisfied and then to ask what relations can therefore be understood to obtain between conceptualized phenomena is to approach the domain of financial theory from the wrong end. Joan Robinson has referred to this theoretical problem and has reproached the contortions in which some analyses have resulted by observing that "it is impossible for a system to *get into* a position of equilibrium, for the very nature of equilibrium is that the system is already in it, and has been in it for a certain length of past time."[54] The theory of financial markets needs now to give attention to the changing behavior of decision makers in the flow of actual time, in the environment of irreducible uncertainty, and in the context of surrounding and continuing changes in economic affairs. Care should be taken not to speak so much of *states* of disequilibrium as opposed to *states* of equilibrium. Instead, when we speak of disequilibrium it will be preferable to envisage not primarily or solely existent and describable *states*, but the complexes of motivations to action and to change, and the pressures to directions of movement, not always quantifiable, that reside in the economic scheme of things.

[54]Joan Robinson, "The Production Function and the Theory of Capital," *Review of Economic Studies* 31 quoted in Coddington, "Creaking Semaphores," p. 157.

2

Inheritance, Convention, and the Contemplation of Change

The theory of financial markets is concerned, essentially though not solely, with the determination at a point in time of the market prices of financial assets. This implies, from the viewpoint of the suppliers of money capital funds, the yields available on portfolios of financial assets or the rates of returns on corporate capital securities; and from the viewpoint of the demanders of money capital it implies the "cost of capital," which influences the corporation's financing mix and its real capital formation decisions.

Money capital is, in a sense, homogeneous; and the allocation of it to the financing in the business firm of different asset installations of different technological capacities, durabilities, and money capital intensities may be regarded as the dehomogenization of money capital.[1] But the notion of the homogeneity of money capital should not be allowed to cloud the importance of the widely diverse *forms* in which it is made available to corporate firms, implying the wide range of heterogeneous capital securities which may be issued and the range of *sources* from which funds might be obtained.

The economic uniqueness of the firm raises a number of questions that must be considered by financial investors who supply capital funds by acquiring the ownership or other securities of corporate firms. Raised here is the importance of what Keynes referred to as "the news," or the significance of the development and emergence of "information" of different degrees of quality, reliability, and significance, and its onward transmission from the real to the financial markets. What this does is to call in question the reliability of the notion that the securities issued by various firms can be homogenized and assumed to be perfectly substitutable for one another simply on the

[1] Cf. Vickers, *Theory of the Firm* pp. 110, 125, 149, and L. M. Lachmann, *Capital and its Structure* (London: G. Bell and Son, 1956), p. 36.

basis of the subjectively assigned probability distributions by which their projected rates of return might be described. Risk, conceived of in this probabilistic sense, is much too narrow a category to be used for classifying disparate, economically unique, and separately identifiable corporate securities and firms.

The postulates of the conventional theory of portfolio selection that a given "investment opportunity set" can be defined exhaustively in terms of the securities' probability characteristics, or that choice is made against stable utility functions defined over risk and return, do themselves fall to the ground. For even if such an "opportunity set" could be specified there would be many reasons why minimal, if any, reliance could be placed on the descriptive stability of it.

The economic uniqueness of the firm, moreover, requires the recognition that decision makers necessarily take, at definable points and in definable environments in locations in historic time, positions determined by what I have labeled in the heading of this chapter as *inheritance.* By inheritance I mean something more than what may be regarded as a wealth endowment, or, in the sense of the Walrasian pure exchange model, a commodity endowment with which the tatonnement market process is entered. Inheritance refers to the total collection of phenomena that describes the givenness of an economic decision maker's situation, and the motivating factors that bear upon that situation.

Suppliers of labor, for example, inherit definable, differential, and marketable skills and corresponding income earning expectations. They are enmeshed in a definable institutional structure which prescribes to a degree their freedom in possible bargaining movement; and they inherit an industrial milieu, mobility potential, and sociocultural canons determined to some degree by that industrial nexus and determining their potential for participation in it. Similarly, the corporate firm inherits a given industrial structure, an existing complex of real assets and production processes, traditions as to pricing policies, enterprise goals, contracts for resource supplies and output sales, management practices and efficiencies. Most important, no doubt, is the givenness of the firm's inheritance of the real capital assets in which money capital has been sunk, with ktheir specificity and immobility, and the delimitation of the firm's freedom for economic maneuver that results. For one of the important features of the industrial scheme of things is that continuous and viable spot markets for second-hand real capital assets do not exist. Similarly, financial investors inherit at any point in time specifiable wealth endowments, savings propensities, expectations, and institutional constraints on the scope for, and the costs of, investment decisions.

While the connotation of the concept of *inheritance* can thus be intuited adequately for ongoing analysis, the concept is itself closely enmeshed with those I have labeled *convention* and the associated *contemplation of change*. These concepts converge on the twofold notion, first, that decision makers always stand at definable temporal, environmental, and knowledge points; and second, that theoretical analysis is primarily concerned not with unchanging continuities but with changes that occur in established situations at such specific points in time. I am concerned with an economics of movement and change, not in the sense of a mathematical dynamic *system*, in which time itself has been reduced to a serially dated logical variable, or in which equilibrium dynamic *paths* may simply have replaced equilibrium *states* without any basic reconstruction of the thought forms employed. Rather, I am interested in change in the sense of the alternative next steps that, in more or less well understood situations, individuals might take to their best advantage.

Economics of Movement

Alfred Marshall, whose *Principles of Economics* is replete with a sense of historic time, was concerned substantially with a grand design of "studying a recognizable economy in a particular phase of its historical development;"[2] and of the "Marshallians" it has been said that "they examined the existing world in a spirit of respect, they brought as much of it intact into their discourse as they could, they valued the contours and features of the landscape they beheld and tried to mold their argument upon them."[3] Marshall should be understood in the light of the caution in which he enveloped his argument:

> But we cannot foresee the future perfectly. The unexpected may happen; and the existing tendencies may be modified before they have had time to accomplish what appears now to be their full and complete work. The fact that the general conditions of life are not stationary is the source of many of the difficulties that are met with in applying economic doctrines to practical problems.[4]

Marshall understood quite clearly that "the unexpected may happen," and financial theory should surely take full account also of the same kind of perspective. If this is done, then the possible outcomes

[2]Joan Robinson, *History versus Equilibrium* (London: Thames Polytechnic, 1974), p. 6.

[3]G. L. S. Shackle, *The Years of High Theory* (Cambridge: Cambridge Univ. Press, 1967), p. 47.

[4]Alfred Marshall, *Principles of Economics*, 9th (variorum) ed. (London: Macmillan, [1920], 1961), p. 347.

in the future that an economic decision maker must contemplate cannot be amenable to complete description in probabilistic terms, for probability descriptions cannot in logic leave any room for the unexpected at all. Probabilistic models necessarily preassign value magnitudes to expectations, which, taken together, exhaustively corral and prescribe what can happen.

Marshall did, of course, simplify parts of his argument by speaking of the "representative firm" and the trees in the forest and indulging in such compressed analytical devices, but these were intellectual constructs designed to accommodate the realities of economic behavior in historic time to what was soon to become, in the hands of his followers, a timeless and static theory.[5] But Marshall's vision is attested by his own prefatory claim that

> the main concern of economics is thus with human beings who are impelled, for good and evil, to change and progress. Fragmentary statical hypotheses are used as temporary auxiliaries to dynamical—or rather biological—conceptions: but *the central ideas of economics,* even when the Foundations alone are under discussion, *must be that of living force and movement.*[6]

His work, as he conceived of it, "is concerned throughout with the *forces that cause movement:* and its keynote is that of dynamics, rather than statics."[7]

"The fact that the assumptions of the static state often underlie present-day economic theory," Keynes was later to say with a clearer prophetic sense than he could then have been aware of, "imports into it a large element of unreality."[8] He was concerned with "bringing it back to reality," and "in general," he was to say, "we have no predominant interest in the *status quo* as such."[9] His perceptions were taken up with "the problems of the real world in which our previous expectations are liable to disappointment and expectations concerning the future affect what we do today."[10] For Keynes too, "equilibrium was

[5]Shackle has remarked perceptively that "Marshall . . . has been accused of lack of rigour. How else, except by a relaxation of rigour, can a compromise between incompatibles be achieved? . . .Marshall . . . resorted to a softening of precision and rigour in the effort to simplify the vast, fluid, elusive maze of the business aspects of human affairs." See Shackle, *Epistemics & Economics*, p. xvii.

[6]Marshall, *Principles of Economics,* p. xv, our italics.

[7]Ibid., p. xiv, our italics. Cf. also the eloquent and well-known passage in the *Principles,* p. 368, in which Marshall discusses the manner in which "in the world in which we live . . . every economic force is constantly changing its action. . . ," and concludes with the probably not completely tongue-in-cheek observation that "a man is likely to be a better economist if he trusts to his commonsense, and practical instincts, than if he professes to study the theory of value and is resolved to find it easy."

[8]Keynes, *General Theory,* p. 146.

[9]Ibid., pp. 146, 243.

[10]Ibid., p. 293-94.

the antithesis of the *General Theory's* inward vision of business life."[11] Indeed Keynes emphasized the direction and manner in which his *General Theory* went beyond his earlier work. His earlier "lack of emancipation from preconceived ideas showed itself," he judged, in its failure "to deal thoroughly with the effects of *changes*. . . ."[12] The *General Theory*, on the other hand, "evolved into what is primarily a study of the forces which determine *changes*. . . ," and "a monetary economy . . . is essentially one in which *changing* views about the future" must be taken fully into account.[13] Keynes expressively referred to a "*shifting* equilibrium," which was "liable to change without much warning, and sometimes substantially."[14]

This perception of change and flux needs to determine also the theory of financial markets. In Chapter 12 of the *General Theory* there is clear recognition that "even apart from the instability due to speculation, there is the instability due to the characteristic of human nature that a large proportion of our positive activities depend on spontaneous optimism rather than on a mathematical expectation, whether moral or hedonistic or economic."[15] Keynes refers to the manner in which "most . . . of our decisions to do something positive" follow from "a spontaneous urge to action . . . and not as the outcome of a weighted average of quantitative benefits multiplied by quantitative probabilities."[16]

To focus on the financial markets, consider, for example, the form of the liquidity preference function, or the demand for money function, as that is normally described by a smooth, southeast-sloping curve in a money-interest rate plane. Surely it is a misunderstanding of Keynes to imagine, in the fashion of the post-Hicksian general equilibrium theoretic representation, that such a functionalized relationship was intended to exhibit a dependably *stable* empirical relationship. Or in the probabilistic and utility theoretic construction of Tobin, it is similarly a mistake to imagine that we have the essence of the Keynesian demand for liquidity and its significance for the determination of the rate of interest.[17]

The instability of the function and its shifts through time led Keynes to the conclusion that

> it is not surprising that the volume of investment . . . should fluctuate widely from time to time. For it depends on two sets of judgments about the

[11]Shackle, *Epistemics & Economics*, p. 435.

[12]Keynes, *General Theory*, p. vii, italics in original.

[13]Ibid., p. vii, my italics.

[14]Ibid., pp. 293, 249, my italics. On this, see the significant analysis in Kregel, "Economic Methodology."

[15]Ibid., p. 161.

[16]Ibid.

[17]Tobin, "Liquidity Preference."

> future, neither of which rests on an adequate or secure foundation—on the propensity to hoard and on opinions of the future yield of capital assets. . . . If, on the other hand, our knowledge of the future was calculable and not subject to sudden changes, it might be justifiable to assume that the liquidity-preference curve was . . . stable.[18]

The determinant functions in the Keynesian scheme are thus not stable in the general equilibrium sense at all. Speculative demands and supplies must be taken into account in explaining variations in the rate of interest and its effects on the rest of the economic system.[19]

Economic Time

In general equilibrium theory time is either assumed away as a theoretical problematic or it enters only as a serially dated logical variable. But time is historic. It is to be understood in an actual calendar sense. It passes. Our awareness of it is deeply bound up with our knowledge and with the knowability of the world in which our decisions have to be made and which, in turn, interacts with our decisions, our imaginations, and our actions in determining outcomes of economic significance to us.

In Marshall's view time stands like a riddle at the core of economic theory, and "the element of time" was "the source of many of the greatest difficulties in economics."[20] But his concern was suppressed by his followers and his viewpoint was transmuted in the 1930s in the manner of Joan Robinson's articulate and influential *Economics of Imperfect Competition*: "The technique set out in this book is a technique for studying equilibrium positions. No reference is made to the effects of the passage of time . . . no study is made of the process of moving from one position of equilibrium to another. . . ."[21] Joan Robinson has referred with candor to her "shameless fudge . . . [by which] comparisons of static equilibrium positions . . . [were] dressed up to appear to represent a process going on through time."[22] It was thus that in the "years of high theory" between Marshall and the Second World War the traditions of static equilibrium analysis were

[18]Keynes, "General Theory of Employment," pp. 218-19.

[19]Our understanding at this point of the significance for Keynes's system of *changes* rather than of static or stable relations might be supplemented by a consideration of the other most neglected chapter in the *General Theory*, chapter 19 on "Changes in Money-Wages." Keynes has presented there not a theory of wages but an argument about *changes* in wages.

[20]Marshall, *Principles of Economics*, p. 109.

[21]Joan Robinson, *The Economics of Imperfect Competition*, 2d ed. (London: Macmillan, [1934] 1969), p. 16.

[22]Ibid., p. vi.

consolidated.[23] In the Hicksian reconstruction of the macroeconomic message of Keynes the analysis of temporal reality was quickly submerged by the same triumphant static tradition. The way that was thereby opened led definitively to a neo-Walrasian reinterpretation of things. Marshall's sensibility to the reality of economic time, and Keynes's own analysis in what was an essentially Marshallian tradition, were subverted to only pale reflections of parts of themselves in the mirror of Walrasian statics and equilibrium.

Keynes, Joan Robinson acknowledges, "brought the argument down from timeless stationary states into the present, here and now, when the past cannot be changed and the future cannot be known."[24] Thus we have to see the decision maker standing in what Shackle has eloquently termed "the solitary moment," locked in the "now" between a "dead yesterday" and an "unborn tomorrow."[25]

> Time and knowledge belong together. . . . The impossibility of prediction in economics follows from the facts that economic change is linked to change in knowledge, and future knowledge cannot be gained before its time. . . . As soon as we permit time to elapse we must permit knowledge to change, and knowledge cannot be regarded as a function of anything else.[26]

The decision maker is what he is, and he knows what he knows, because of the process of time through which he has come to his present temporal point. Inescapably he stands at his solitary decision point with that collection of prejudices, predilections, presuppositions, and preferences that have been temporally and socioculturally conditioned and formed. The decision maker's environmental conditions have been determined and are what they are because they too have partaken in the same historically or temporally determined process.[27] There exists an institutionally structured capitalist system, an industrial, corporate, and market complex, a pattern of wealth and ownership distribution, capital and savings congealed in

[23]Cf. Shackle, *Years of High Theory* pp. 47-48.

[24]Joan Robinson, *Economic Heresies* (New York: Basic Books, 1971), p. ix.

[25]G. L. S. Shackle, *Decision, Order and Time in Human Affairs* (Cambridge: Cambridge University Press, 1969), pp. 14ff; cf. Schackle, *Epistemics & Economics*, p. xi.

[26]Ludwig M. Lachmann, in *Econometrica* 11 (1959), quoted in Shackle, *Decision, Order and Time*, p. 41. Professor Shackle's extensive work has illumined this area of analysis, particularly his scintillating encapsulization of it in his *Decision, Order and Time in Human Affairs*.

[27]It might be observed that to conceive in this way of the identifiable moment in time and its determination by the confluence of historical processes antecedent to it in no way calls in question whatever ontological meaning is to be understood as lying behind that temporal process itself, and we do not in any sense disallow Shakespeare's dictum, for example, that "There's a divinity that shapes our ends, roughhew them how we will," *Hamlet* Act 5, Scene 2, line 10.

physical and productive assets, and a structure of earnings and welfare expectations.

Behavioral actions and patterns observed at any time are what they are because they occur at *that* point in time and not at some *other* point. The "moment in being" is unique, uniquely conditioned, and, in the nature of the case, is past beyond recapture when it has gone.[28] It is not in any logical sense repeatable, and it is incapable therefore of ever again providing precisely the same decision nexus as that which it once bequeathed. For economics, decision situations are clearly nonrepetitive, and extensive lines of intertemporal comparisons are rendered suspect if not meaningless. For every historic moment has its own being, its own history, its own inheritance, and its own knowledge complex.

My arguments thus point toward the logical inadmissibility of comparison tests between the supposed efficiency of decisions at points in time at which they occur on the one hand, and the outcomes following from those decisions at definable subsequent points in time on the other. The decision at one point in time and the outcome at another point can of course be observed and recorded; and the outcome at *its* point in time will contribute in its own unique way to the economic individual's inheritance, decision alternatives, and possible courses of action *at that same* point of time. But that in no sense imparts any meaning at all to the "ex ante, ex post" comparison that I have just characterized as logically inadmissible. For at the posterior point in time the economic individual, even if only in the matter of historically generated knowledge, is a "different" economic individual from what he must, for the purposes in hand, have been at the anterior point in time.

The worthwhileness of an economic decision can therefore be assessed by the decision maker only with reference to the degree of complacency, or satisfaction, or ease or repose of mind the decision provides *at the time at which it is made*. This should enable us to grasp also the same uniqueness and nonrepetitive character of the decision alternatives themselves. Capital investment expenditures in the business firm are an important case in point. Every such decision must necessarily change what would otherwise have been the "inheritance" of every subsequent possible decision moment. Shackle has referred in this connection to *self-destructive* decisions or experiments. There are certain kinds of decisions such that after them,

> there can be no going back to the state of affairs which prevailed while the choice was still open. . . . It is, accordingly, logically impossible for a person

[28] Shackle, *Decision, Order and Time*, pp. 38, 40.

> who has to make a decision in such an instance to contemplate *repeating* his experiment: such experiments are self-destructive . . . for he cannot be made to unlearn his new knowledge and unlive his experience. . . . The one-way traffic of human history allows no repetition of the kinds of experiment which change men's ideas. They are self-destructive experiments.[29]

The nonrepetitiveness of such unique decision events points to the inadmissibility of the probabilistic description of the possible outcomes of the unique decisions or actions.

Historic time must inform financial theory, not only by reason of the temporal inheritance or the actual time of decision making itself, but because of the implications *for* the decision and *for* market behavior of the results and processes which will occur in historic time *after* the decision event. It is in this respect that financial theory, as it aspires to real world contiguity, needs now to recapture the Keynesian design of discussing the world in the spirit of Marshall's respect for time. It is basic to the message of the *General Theory* not only that the future is unknown, but that production takes time. Because production, along with earning and spending and saving and investing, takes place in time, there is nothing inherent in the system to guarantee that false trades and false production will not occur. There is nothing to guarantee that actual income and wealth realizations accord with the hopes and expectations that first gave rise to action and formed the constraints in terms of which initial decisions were made.

Time admits of error also because real capital assets generally have long gestation periods and long economic lives. The uncertainty that results from this, the distrust of the future with which fixed investment is surrounded, induces a search for safety in the demand for liquid assets, and money thus has a place in the scheme of things. For the fixity of the production process, the fixedness of certain costs and the hoped-for realization of a target rate of return on invested money capital raise the possibility that corporate cash flow streams might not be of a level and time shape necessary to preserve solvency in the firm. The implied uncertainty may be distributed throughout the corporate and industrial system by arrangements of contract.[30] In almost all labor markets, for example, inputs to the firm are acquired on a basis of forward contracts, and the manner in which the firm reacts to changes in demand or cost variations by price or output adjustments will depend on the structure of cost and revenue contractual arrangements that exist.

[29] Ibid., pp. 56-57, italics in original.

[30] Cf. the valuable discussion of contractual arrangements in Davidson, *Money and the Real World*, passim.

Historic time is relevant also to the economic as distinct from the technological life of real capital assets to which the firm's investable money capital is committed. It is here that the theory of optimum investment decision making or optimum capital budgeting enters the analysis. Another example, significant for the financial markets and for portfolio investment opportunities on the one hand, and for the cost and mix of corporate capital securities from the firm's point of view on the other, is that of the maturity horizons of securities issued in exchange for money capital funds.

Realized time horizons are relevant in several respects. First, the realized holding periods of investment positions in the financial markets determine the rates of return actually realized on such positions, and the possibility of realized capital gains or losses has implications for changes in asset value endowments, for "inheritances," and for ongoing economic decisions. Second, the variability of the holding period of portfolio positions strikes at the explanatory significance of the equilibrium theory of financial asset pricing. For the speculative variation of the holding period sets up the likelihood of false trading in the financial markets, with implications for wealth endowment effects, asset value redistribution effects, and variations in market prices, yields, and the costs of money capital funds.

Economics of Convention

Against the background of inheritance and of change, we can consider the significant notion of *convention* in economic affairs and in market behavior. Conventions may change, and they may change quite suddenly, but they nevertheless exist at points in time, and they do lend an orderedness to the economic patterns of things.

Keynes has brought the question into analytical focus: "How do we manage in such circumstances to behave in a manner which saves our faces as rational, economic men?"[31] He saw acutely in Chapter 12 of the *General Theory* the speculative character of day-to-day Stock Exchange activity, and he espoused the interpretative notion of *conventional valuation.* His explanation of the restlessness of the market, in which he enjoyed considerable success, was that speculators were engaged in trying to guess or imagine what would be the opinion later in the day or the month or the year of the majority of their fellow speculators. On this important argument Shackle observes, "A valuation which is arrived at by a speculative market whose members are

[31]Keynes, "General Theory of Employment," p. 214.

trying to guess the forthcoming opinion of their own majority is what Keynes calls a *conventional* valuation."[32]

Keynes similarly explained the rate of interest as a "highly conventional variable," dependent substantially on a speculative demand for liquidity.[33] And this "inherently restless variable" is to a large degree dependent at any time on market *conventional* expectations as to what the rate should be.[34] This in turn places limits on the effectiveness of monetary policy in moving the rate. For the speculative and restless character of the market for liquidity could not be disciplined into the smooth and stable function of the static argument, even if it were specified by a utility-probability theoretic argument in the manner of Tobin.

But economic and financial market decisions have perforce to be made, and they must be based on something. Keynes advanced the notion that at any point in time they reflect "what we may strictly term a *conventional* judgment." In given situations "we assume that the present is a . . . serviceable guide to the future. . . . We assume that the *existing* state of opinion as expressed in prices and the character of existing output is based on a *correct* summing up of future prospects, *so that we can accept it as such until something new and relevant comes into the picture*."[35] Of course this may be a "flimsy foundation," and it may be "subject to sudden and violent changes." But it nevertheless provides a basis for continuity in economic and market affairs which imparts at least a quasi-stability to behavior at large. We are inclined to accept the conventional, Keynes observed, "until something new and relevant comes into the picture."

A Model of Pricing and Output Policy

But in actual fact there are reasons deeper than convention, reasons underlying the formation of conventions, for degrees of stability in the system. Consider, for example, the determinants of price formation in the industrial firm. This has relevance for financial market theory by reason of its incorporation of required rates of return on money capital investment, and the ability of the firm to produce internally generated cash flows as a partial source of its financing requirements. To the extent that corporate cash flows become available for capital invest-

[32]Shackle, *Epistemics & Economics*, p. 223, italics in original. See Shackle's further discussion in Chapter 21 on "Prices as Convention."

[33]Keynes, *General Theory*, p. 203.

[34]Shackle, *Epistemics & Economics*, p. 199.

[35]Keynes, "General Theory of Employment," p. 214, italics partially supplied.

ment financing, to the extent that the demand pressures on external financial markets are alleviated, variations occur in firms' debt-to-equity financing ratios, affecting the degrees of risk to which the suppliers of external funds are exposed and thereby the costs of money capital of different kinds.

In Figure 1, *APC* refers to average prime costs, *MPC* indicates marginal prime costs, and *ATC* refers to average total costs. The latter curve will have superimposed on prime costs the required or target or "normal" rate of return on the money capital at work in the firm. When the firm has assessed its operating cost relationships, its task is then to estimate the amounts of output buyers could be expected to demand at prices just equal to the firm's average total cost of production. These amounts are described by the estimated demand curve *DD*. Then the producer knows that, according to estimates, if he produces an output quantity of *OA* and sells it at the unit price of $AC = OH$ he will cover all operating costs and achieve his target return on capital employed. If the estimated demand curve assumed the locus D_1D_1, the firm could choose between the production points adjacent to *M* and *N*, both of which would provide the target rates of return on capital.

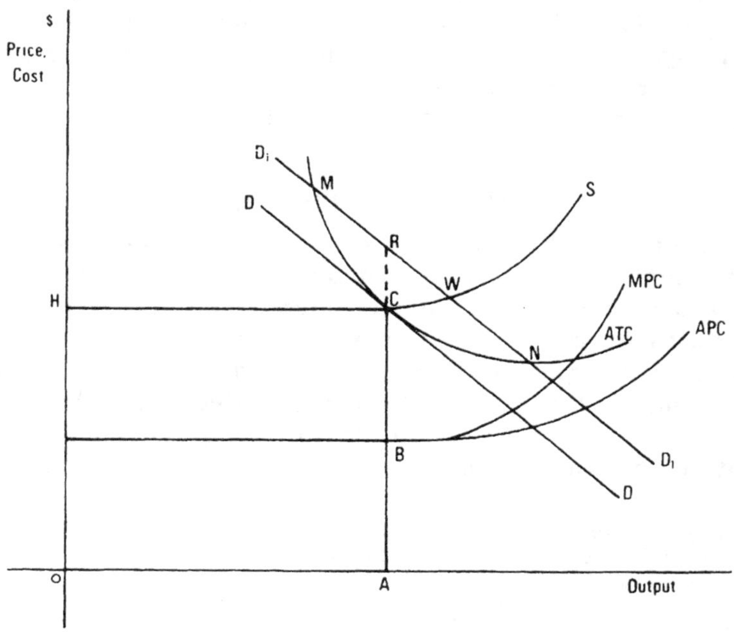

Figure 1.

The output volume *OA* can be referred to as the "standard volume" of output. At this standard volume the producer has in effect determined his selling price by "marking up" his prime costs of *AB* by a unit gross profit margin of *BC* to provide the desired return on the capital stock employed. It follows that once the firm's production technique, its capital investment, and its potential revenues have been specified, and once the operating structure of the firm and its standard production volume have been decided upon, the firm's short-period output supply curve can be described. This is indicated by the curve *HS* in Figure 1. When the operating arrangements have been established, the short-run supply curve will be perfectly elastic until capacity output volume is reached, provided only that the prices of factors of production that enter into prime cost remain constant.

The *ATC* curve of the firm can be regarded as describing only the *potential* supply prices for given output levels until the standard production volume for the short-run operating period has been decided upon. But *after* this standard volume operating decision has been made, and *after* the production arrangements of the firm have been agreed upon, *then* the short-run supply curve is as described by *HS*, in which the mark-up over prime costs at standard volume is incorporated.

It follows then that if the firm should experience a decline in demand, the demand curve will move to the left (not shown in the diagram) and will intersect the horizontal supply curve between *H* and *C*. The firm's selling price will remain fixed and its output volume will fall. The firm will then be maintaining its unit profit-margin mark-up on unit standard costs, but it will fail to realize the total return on capital on the basis of which it established its standard volume of production in the first place. In such a case the *realized rate* of return on capital employed will fall below its target level, and if the reduction in demand should be judged to be permanent the firm can be expected to reallocate its capital, so far as it is mobile, to alternative uses.

Conversely, if demand conditions should improve an opposite reaction may be expected. If the demand rose from *DD* to D_1D_1, the short-run price and output volume would be described by the coordinates of point *W*. If this new intersection point should occur at a production volume below capacity there will be no change in selling price, but an increase in production volume will occur. But in the change in demand conditions shown in Figure 1 the new demand price for standard volume *OA* is actually *AR*, which exceeds the supply price for that volume by *CR*. This implies that there is now potentially available to the firm a larger than target return on its capital investment. If the firm expects the favorable demand conditions to continue permanently it will be motivated to expand its capital investment.[36]

Thus a new confrontation between the firm and the financial market occurs, an new financing and capital security issues will take place. The supply-and-demand postures in the financial asset market are disturbed, the financial investors' "asset investment opportunity set" has been augmented, and new asset pricing conditions can be expected to eventuate.

This entire argument regarding firm behavior points in the direction of short-run price stability in large sections of manufacturing industry. It is an analytical underpinning of Keynes' assumption that "conventional" expectations do surround given price structures in the economy. In the short run it is the firm's supply curve that is perfectly elastic, and not its demand curve as is assumed in the standard competitive Walrasian model. At the theoretical level this conclusion departs from the assumption of infinite price-adjustment velocities contained in the neo-Walrasian general equilibrium argument.

This pricing and output model provides also the microeconomic foundation for the "shifting" employment, output, and national income equilibrium with which Keynes in his macroeconomic analysis was preeminently concerned.[37] The theory also opens the prospect of false trading in commodity markets. In general, false trading can be expected to be pervasive.

On this argument, the implication of false trading is that variations may occur in realized and anticipated rates of return on capital investment, providing a direct linkage between the present discussion and the theory of financial market behavior. Moreover, false trading in

[36]The foregoing argument is indebted to Davidson, *Money and the Real World,* pp. 37-40. Davidson observes that "this standard volume-target return pricing approach has been found to be the predominant method used by management in such major industries as aluminium, automobiles, chemicals and steel," and he refers to W. Adams, *The Structure of American Industry* (New York: Macmillan, 1961). See also Alfred S. Eichner and J. A. Kregel, "An Essay on Post-Keynesian Theory: A New Paradigm in Economics," *Journal of Economic Literature* 13 (December 1975). A further view of price and quantity adjustment processes is contained in Paul Davidson, "Disequilibrium Market Adjustment: Marshall Revisited," *Economic Inquiry* (June, 1974).

[37]Cf. Donald J. Harris, "The Price Policy of Firms, the Level of Employment and the Distribution of Income in the Short Run," *Australian Economic Papers* 13 (June 1974), for a valuable discussion and summary of theories of wage-cost mark-ups; and A. S. Eichner, "A Theory of the Determination of the Mark-up under Oligopoly," *Economic Journal* 83 (December 1973). Further perspective can be found in P. Wiles, "Cost Inflation and the State of Economic Theory," *Economic Journal* 83 (1973) and in the exchange of comments on this article by G. C. Means, A. Nove, S. Weintraub, and P. Wiles, in the June 1974 issue of the same *Journal.* See also Paul Davidson and Sidney Weintraub, "Money as Cause and Effect," *Economic Journal* 83 (December 1973), for a discussion of the mark-up question and perceptive comments on some relevant theory in relation to Walrasian general equilibrium models.

the real markets of the economy can be expected to transmit false or misleading information to the financial markets, giving rise to false trading in the latter markets also. When to these possible outcomes is added the phenomenon of purely speculative trading in the financial markets, reasons accumulate to call in question the real world relevance of the conventional theory of financial asset prices. To take only one case in point: did any false trading occur in the financial asset markets during the first two months of 1977, when the difference between the high and the low level of the Dow-Jones Industrial Average on the New York Stock Exchange was 67 points? Did any change in "wealth endowment" or any wealth redistribution effect occur during that period, when some seven percent of existing common stock portfolio values was destroyed? Do changes of a similar kind, if not of the same magnitude, occur in the market at other times?

Economic Change

My analysis has been based on a given or definite cost function as envisaged by the firm. Although the argument has been conducted in terms of administered prices, its scope transcends this restriction. For example, if the firms are competitive price-takers facing perfectly elastic demand curves they will engage in the same cost type calculations and plan their production volumes accordingly. The firm's profit margin will continue to be the market price P minus the ordinate HS supply curve point. Profit will again be equal to $(P - HS)Q$, where Q refers to the output sales volume.

Inducements to change in the system may follow variations in the firm's cost conditions, arising from changing technological efficiencies or increases in factor prices. Cost-push inflationary conditions, for example, may have become widespread in the economy and may perhaps have been validated by official monetary policy. Over the longer pull, the stock exchange values of firms' securities, or the financial market values of the firms' assets, will tend to be raised toward current replacement values. In all such cases the pricing policies of firms should seek to preserve either rates of return on the book values of capital invested or rates of return on market values.[38] The reactions of individual firms are likely to depend on the degree of real capital intensity in their production processes, their perceived elasticities of demand for their output, their market share and product mix, and on

[38]Robin Marris, *The Economic Theory of Managerial Capitalism* (London: Macmillan, 1964), p. 22, refers to "the ratio of the market value of the firm to the book value of its net assets" as the "valuation ratio" and provides a valuable discussion of relevant issues.

the history of financial market attitudes to their capital securities. The behavior response of firms will depend also on the nature of the expectations and the degree of confidence with which those expectations are held, regarding their own future income-generating ability and their need to make claims on the financial markets for additional funds to support their activity and contemplated development.

But considerable evidence suggests a reasonably stable economy-wide prime cost mark-up ratio.[39] Weintraub has capsuled the price determination forces in the expression

$$P = kw/A, \tag{1}$$

where P refers to a general index of prices in the market sector, w refers to the average nominal wage rate, A is a measure of average productivity per unit of labor input to the economic production process, and k describes the prime cost mark-up ratio.[40] Focusing our attention on the possible time rates of change in prices, it follows that

$$lnP = lnk + lnw - lnA, \tag{2}$$

and assuming a constant mark-up factor,

$$\frac{1}{P}\frac{dP}{dt} = \frac{1}{w}\frac{dw}{dt} - \frac{1}{A}\frac{dA}{dt} \tag{3}$$

or

$$\dot{P} = \dot{w} - \dot{A}. \tag{4}$$

The final expression suggests that the rate of increase in prices will depend on the simultaneous rates of change in nominal wage rates and the average productivity of labor.[41]

This microeconomic price level formulation thus brings into focus also the directions from which relations emerge between the indus-

[39]Cf. Sidney Weintraub, *A General Theory of the Price Level, Output, Income Distribution and Economic Growth* (Philadelphia: Chilton, 1959) and *Keynes and the Monetarists* (New Brunswick: Rutgers University Press, 1973) for the most thorough development of this and related arguments and for the examination of their implications, both for inflationary phenomena in capitalist economies and for appropriate aggregative economic policies.

[40]It should be noted, however, that Weintraub does not interpret this as simply a "cost-push" or "wage-push" formulation. He points out that wages and salaries comprise about 90 percent of consumer demand so that when average employee compensation, w, increases, product demand curves move to the right. Likewise, small oscillations in k are taken to reflect overall demand phenomena.

[41]Cf. a comparable explanatory equation which takes account also of changes in import prices in J. A. Trevithick and C. Mulvey, *The Economics of Inflation* (New York: Wiley, 1975), p. 79. See also Sidney Weintraub, "Inflation in the World Economy," *Kyklos*, 1977, and, for the consumer sector argument especially, his *Capitalism's Inflation and Unemployment Crisis* (Reading, Pa.: Addison-Wesley, 1977), chapter 3.

trial firm and its pricing, cash flow, and investment policies on the one hand and the financial markets and macroeconomic stability on the other.

The Inducement to Invest

The model described in Figure 1 has implicitly indicated the conditions under which the firm can be expected to undertake additional investment expenditures. Its prime cost mark-up factor could be set at a level designed to generate a part of its anticipated normal financing requirements, and for the remainder of those needs it will approach the financial asset market with newly issued capital securities. Let us imagine now that in its anticipation of its trading revenue the firm has focused its attention on a particular level. We might refer to this as R_t, its *focus value* revenue in period t. If, however a more favorable demand pattern emerged as envisaged in Figure 1, or if the firm were favorably "surprised" by a revenue stream, $R_t + \Delta R_t$, which exceeded its focus expectation, it may be forced to reevaluate its real capital requirements in the light of its need to meet a higher level of demand in the future. In such a case we can then observe in the emergence of favorable trading results both a *motivation* to increased real capital formation and, by reason of the larger internally generated cash flow, a *facilitation* of the new investment it might be decided to make.

To the extent that the incremental investment requires new issues of capital securities, the firm will be interested in the reaction of the financial markets to its favorable trading results and its expansion prospects. The retention of its internally generated cash flow will increase the amount of equity ownership funds in the firm, and the consequent reduction of the debt-to-equity ratio will diminish the financial risk exposure of the security holders. On the not unreasonable assumption or risk-aversion on the supply side of the financial markets, these beneficial developments will tend to lower the firm's cost of money capital funds.[42]

Thus it is that the background and motivation of the firm's confrontation with the financial markets instances the need in financial theory for a clear understanding of the step-by-step changes that take place in the actual round of affairs. I will turn in the next chapter to a fuller discussion of the firm's relation with its external financing market.

[42]Relevant financial data may be inspected in any recent issue of the *Economic Report of the President* (Washington: U.S. Government Printing Office). In 1974, for example, total sources of funds for "nonfarm nonfinancial corporate business" amounted to U.S.$183 billion, of which $81 billion or 44 percent was obtained from internal sources, including undistributed profits and depreciation allowances, and $102 billion or 56 percent came from external sources. In that year, of $77 billion raised from new security issues, 95 percent was in the form of new debt issues.

3

The Firm and its Financial Market Dependence

The setting of the financial markets in "the capitalist process" brings into prominence the terms on which money capital funds become available to borrowers, in particular to the suppliers of corporate capital securities. By determining the "cost of capital," this influences directly the process of real capital formation in the economy. In this chapter, I examine more fully the conditions on the demand side of the money capital markets, and the issues involved in incremental investment in the firm will be sharpened to lead to an economic worthwhileness criterion in terms of "the full marginal cost of relaxing the firm's money capital availability constraint."

Production, Investment, and Finance

The pricing and output model in the preceding chapter investigated the short-run behavior of the firm under the assumption that a specified amount of money capital had been committed to it. The current price-output decision contemplated the adequacy of the actual earnings generated on this capital endowment. My focus now turns to the anterior question of evaluating the *ab initio* structural planning of the firm as a whole. In more familiar terminology, I am concerned now with the long run as distinct from the short run, and the analysis invokes the familiar proposition that given sufficient time all factor inputs are variable. For purposes of the present argument, therefore, financial capital is not yet presumed to have been committed to the necessary real capital installations of machinery, buildings, and productive equipment in general.

There is also less need to distinguish between the short and the long run in terms of lengths of calendar time. The distinction between the short and the long run is at this stage primarily a matter of viewpoint. In one case, the point of view adopted by the management of the firm is that from which, in the presence of a technologically established productive apparatus, decisions relate to the unit price at which its output will be offered on the market. Unit costs and capacity are constrained by inherited production facilities. In the other case, the management examines the various technologically possible ways of doing things and chooses the most effective in the light of its projected product mix. Given the money capital requirements implied by the different real capital intensities of the alternative production processes, it selects those specific arrangements that promise to be economically optimal.

Nevertheless, the short-run model already presented remains vital, and it points in the direction from which the capital investment problem comes into perspective. In the earlier case, the average total cost (*ATC*) curve was interpreted as a *potential* locus of price and output coordinates, and with a given set of productive resources at its disposal the firm was able to choose any point on that locus *until it had determined its "standard volume" of output* and had allocated its costs and prices accordingly. But once the standard volume was decided upon and actual operations were set under way, the short-run supply curve was understood to assume the form we indicated as *HS* in Figure 1. Now from the long-run viewpoint, and pushing our perspective back to the prior question of the technological organization of the firm, the management must incorporate as a planning input the target return it judges to be adequate to justify the choice of whatever capital installations it selects from among the available alternatives.

At the stage of *ab initio* structural enterprise planning, the money capital available to the firm, either from the owners' resources or from the financial market, can potentially be congealed in any of a number of technologically feasible real capital arrangements, or in plants described by different technological "blueprints." Profitability criteria will point to one particular and optimum arrangement. It might or might not be one that would be easily adaptable in the future to producing outputs other than those initially in view, or to being put to alternative economic uses. Optimum technological planning, that is to say, may provide for varying degrees of flexibility, mobility, or specificity in the contemplated real productive assets, or in the different forms of congealed money capital resources.

Flexibility in real capital planning may contain advantages because there do not in general exist continuous and viable markets for second-hand real capital assets. From the economic-financial and from the technological points of view, capital that can be regarded as "putty" from the *ab initio* planning view becomes "clay" from the point of view of the ongoing concern after its operations have actually been set in motion.

These considerations have implications that spill over into the money capital or financial asset markets. They introduce a riskiness and the prospect of income-uncertainty to the firm and to the purchasers of its securities, thereby influencing the cost of its money capital and the amount of funds it will be able to command in the market. This will also influence the debt-equity mix in which those capital funds will be able to be acquired from risk-averse suppliers.

A structural planning model of the firm needs to bring into relation with each other the different levels of decision problems the firm confronts at this stage.[1] But economic theory has not addressed itself extensively to the significant linkages existing between the factor employment and technological considerations on the one hand, and the firm's confrontation with the money capital market on the other. I have therefore proposed an interdependent trilogy of the firm's optimization decision problems on the levels of production, capital investment, and finance.

Significant work has been done, by Vernon Smith for example, in relation to the first two legs of this trilogy. Smith's main interest was in developing "a unified theory of production and investment."[2] And other authors have more recently considered the last two legs of the trilogy, the investment and financing problems. Lerner and Carleton, for example, noted the lack of a "widely accepted theoretical apparatus linking the market valuation of common stock to a corporation's investment-opportunities schedule, dividend pay-out function, and capital structure."[3] Their analytical procedure was "to depart from the single-equation convention and explicitly introduce two equations: an investment-opportunities (or capital budgeting) schedule and a stock-valuation equation."[4]

But while Smith addressed the trilogy's first two legs and Lerner and Carleton the last two, economic theory has not adequately explored the interdependence between the trilogy of issues I have thus opened up. Since the Smith-Lerner-Carleton work appeared, there have been several efforts to explore the investment and financing connections in the context of the general equilibrium theory of the

[1]A more extensive analysis appears in my *Theory of the Firm;* in "The Cost of Capital and the Structure of the Firm," *Journal of Finance* 25 (March 1970): 35-46; "Disequilibrium Structures"; and "Financial Theory of the Firm" in Sidney Weintraub, ed., *Modern Economic Thought* (Philadelphia: Univ. of Pennsylvania Press, 1977).

[2]Vernon L. Smith, *Investment and Production: A Study in the Theory of the Capital-using Enterprise* (Cambridge: Harvard Univ. Press, 1961), p. vii.

[3]Eugene M. Lerner and Willard T. Carleton, "The Integration of Capital Budgeting and Stock Valuation," *American Economic Review* 54 (September 1964).

[4]Ibid. Cf. also Lerner and Carleton, *A Theory of Financial Analysis* (New York: Harcourt, Brace and World, 1966).

financial asset market.[5] Nevertheless, what has been generally avoided thus far is an examination of the manner in which the firm's confrontation with the money capital market is embedded in the technological structure of its productive processes and its employment of real and money capital-intensive factors of production.

Haley and Schall, whose work is the most distinguished recent examination of the field, and Bierman and Hass discuss the capital investment decision of the firm within the general equilibrium framework.[6] The latter authors invoke the assumptions that "(1) the [securities] market is currently in equilibrium (2) the market will move toward equilibrium if a disequilibrium condition sets in and (3) the market finds out about [the firm's real investment] decision immediately it is made."[7] Consistently with the conventional theory as expounded by Haley and Schall, Bierman and Hass conclude that in the firm's investment decision "the relevant risk consideration is the relation of the risk of the investment to the market risk. *The firm's risk position is not relevant*."[8] In this it would appear that analytical nihilism is triumphant. Apparently, in the theory of the structure of the firm there is no longer any need for the firm at all.

Following a different line of analysis, Arzac has recently produced an argument based explicitly on my *Theory of the Firm*, which, he says, "extends Vickers' analysis by allowing business risk to depend on production and investment decisions."[9] But the analysis contains an excessive concentration on the *optimum optimorum* structural posture of the firm, the situation in which its production, asset investment, and financing structures had been brought to mutually determined optimum positions.[10] Arzac has examined the principal conclu-

[5]Cf. Stewart C. Myers, "Interactions of Corporate Financing and Investment Decisions—Implications for Capital Budgeting," *Journal of Finance*, 29 (March 1974), and on a more designedly quasi-operational level, Clement G. Krouse, "Optimal Financing and Capital Structure Programs for the Firm," *Journal of Finance* 27 (December 1972), L. J. Merville and L. A. Travis, "A Generalized Model for Capital Investment," *Journal of Finance* 28 (March 1973), and James R. Morris, "An Application of the Decomposition Principle to Financial Decision Models," *Journal of Financial and Quantitative Analysis* (March 1975). See also Jensen, *Studies in Capital Markets*, and the bibliography on pp. 41-43. See also Marshall Blume and Irwin Friend, "A New Look at the Capital Asset Pricing Model," *Journal of Finance* 28 (March 1973).

[6]Haley and Schall, *Theory of Financial Decisions*, and Bierman and Hass, *Introduction to Managerial Finance*.

[7]Bierman and Hass, *Introduction to Managerial Finance*, p. 230, parentheses added.

[8]Harold Bierman, Jr., and Jerome E. Hass, "Capital Budgeting under Uncertainty: A Reformulation," *Journal of Finance* 28 (March 1973): 119-29, my italics. Further perspective on this conclusion will be obtained in the discussion in Chapter 6 of the implications for financing decisions of the equilibrium asset pricing theory.

[9]Enrique R. Arzac, "Structural Planning under Controllable Business Risk," *Journal of Finance* 30 (December 1975): 1229-37.

[10]Cf. my *Theory of the Firm* chapter 10, as extended in "The Cost of Capital and the Structure of the Firm."

sions of the equilibrium capital asset pricing model of Sharpe, Lintner, Hamada and others, and has concluded that the Vickers-Arzac investment criterion "is shown to be [a] generalization of theirs, and of the one obtained by Modigliani and Miller under the constant risk class assumption."[11]

But it is necessary to go beyond the analysis of equilibrium structures and equilibrium conditions. For the theory of equilibrium asset prices is too weak a reed to have the weight of the theory of the firm placed upon it when the firm is viewed in the aspect of its changing behavior through time. The need is for a theory which can throw light on behavior in *dis*equilibrium situations.[12]

It is possible, of course, to specify analytical conditions under which interdependencies between production, investment, and financing decisions can be assumed not to hold, and under which, therefore, certain so-called "separation theorems" may be invoked. But if this is done the cost in realism and relevance of the analysis is high. Fama and Miller argue, for example, as follows:

> The major results with respect to the nature of optimal production-financing decisions by firms . . . for a certainty world are the two separation principles . . . (1) *given its production decisions,* a firm's financing decisions are a matter of indifference to its security holders, so that production and financing decisions are separable; and (2) optimal production decisions for a firm simply involve adherence to the market value rule, so that such decisions are independent of the details of owner tastes. . . . *These separation or independence principles hold also in a world of uncertainty,* and in fact their validity requires only the assumed existence of a perfect capital market.[13]

It might reasonably be thought, on the contrary, that to the extent that analysis aspires to real-world relevance it should properly call in question the assumptions and the "givens" in arguments such as these.

[11]Arzac, "Structural Planning," p. 1229.

[12]Arzac, however, is on solid ground when he concludes that the criterion he has derived "is valid only at what Vickers has called the optimum optimorum position of the firm. It requires an optimal financial structure. Under conditions of equity capital rationing, the average cost of capital is irrelevant and for planning purposes should be replaced by the full marginal cost of debt" (Ibid., p. 1236). And "as Vickers has pointed out, the use of the average cost of capital is inappropriate at infra-optimum level of equity" (Ibid., p. 1232). The notion of the infra-optimum disequilibrium position is examined in the next section of this chapter. Cf. my "The Cost of Capital and the Structure of the Firm," and the recognition of the same point in Myers, "Interactions of Corporate Financing and Investment Decisions."

[13]Fama and Miller, *Theory of Finance,* p. 145, my italics. Cf. also Hirschleifer, *Investment, Interest and Capital,* pp. 312, 204, where, in relation to similar conclusions, he refers to "the beautiful Fisherian result . . . Fisher's Separation Theorem."

The Cost of Money Capital

The question confronting the imperfectly competitive firm, and still awaiting resolution in economic theory, is the following: what, in actual fact, is the firm, such as we described in Figure 1 of the preceding chapter, to understand as its cost of money capital for investment decision making purposes? For the main part the theoretical literature has answered the question by specifying the firm's "weighted average cost of capital," or the average cost of the firm's debt capital on the one hand and its equity or ownership capital on the other, where each such capital cost is weighted by the relative importance of the corresponding source of capital in the firm's total capital structure, the weights being measured at market values rather than at the firm's book or balance sheet values. Argument has ensued regarding the stability or otherwise of such a weighted average measure of the cost of money capital, and the considerable and impressive body of work stemming from the seminal Modigliani and Miller paper has lent distinguished support to the proposition that the weighted average cost of capital is invariant with respect to the firm's financing mix or debt-to-equity financing ratio.[14] If the facts of the real world did support such a financing irrelevance theorem, then the way would be open to the empirical reliance on the so-called "separation theorems," and production, investment, and financing decisions could be taken independently of each other.

Attention needs to be given, however, to the interdependencies in the firm's actual decision processes. In a very relevant sense, Oskar Lange in 1936 dissented from the then received traditions in the theory of the firm.[15] The theory then stood, he argued, on the unrealistic assumption that the firm, in making its production and factor use decisions, did not face any shortage of money capital. Lange referred to this as the assumption of "money capital saturation," or the hypothesis that the firm always had sufficient money capital to produce any desired level of output with any desired combination of factor inputs. But we can argue, on the other hand, that the firm should be envisaged not as proceeding toward an unconstrained optimization decision in this manner, but as concerned to achieve its interdependent structural decision outcomes against a "money capital availability constraint."[16] Operatively, therefore, the conditions on which money

[14]Cf. Modigliani and Miller, "Cost of Capital."

[15]Oskar Lange, "The Place of Interest in the Theory of Production," *Review of Economic Studies* 3 (June 1936).

[16]Cf. Vickers, *Theory of the Firm* chapter 6 for a discussion of "The issues in historical perspective."

capital is available to the firm exert significant effects on its optimum production and factor employment decisions.[17]

The less than perfect elasticity of their money capital supply functions is a significant feature of the decision situations confronting firms in their disequilibrium postures in actual market conditions. The "cost of capital" to the firm, then, can be uniquely defined as "the full marginal cost of relaxing the money capital availability constraint." In the general case, decision makers will react to an increased severity of this finance availability constraint by adopting production structures which economize on relatively more money capital-intensive factors.[18] The financing constraint may be relaxed by introducing additional debt or additional equity capital to the firm, and this calls in question the logical cogency and the empirical viability of the widely espoused "weighted average cost of capital." For the weighted average cost of capital is not generally usable as a valid investment decision criterion at all, at least not in the straightforward sense supposed by the relevant theory. It is only when the firm has been brought to its uniquely optimum structural posture that the conventional weighted average cost of capital does in fact equal the cost of relaxing the money capital availability constraint. And in such a posture the average capital cost equals *both* the "full marginal cost of debt" and the "full marginal cost of equity."[19]

If, however, *the analysis is to be locked into its equilibrium theoretic mold*, it follows that the condition in which the weighted average cost of capital has *analytical* relevance and validity is that in which the firm, in all of its optimization decision areas, has been brought to its mutually determined, optimally structured posture. And once the firm *is* at that point optimally structured, no further investment would be contemplated. Hence the only situation in which the average cost of capital is valid and relevant is one in which it would not have to be used.

The firm's objective or maximand function for planning purposes describes the attainable economic value of its ownership shares, understood as the capitalized value of the realizable residual earnings, or as $V = \pi(1 - t)/\rho$. Here the residual income variable, π, denotes the net earnings before tax generated by the firm; t indicates the firm's average tax rate; and the capitalization rate, or the owners' required rate of return, ρ, is functionally dependent on the degree of risk to

[17]Cf. Ibid., passim, for a fuller discussion.

[18]Cf. Vickers, "Cost of Capital and Structure of the Firm," reprinted in L. R. Amey, ed., *Readings in Management Decision* (London: Longman, 1973).

[19]Cf. Ibid., and the acknowledgement and discussion of this point in Arzac, "Structural Planning."

which the owners are exposed. Assuming for the present that the degree of stability in the firm's net operating income stream, or its so-called "business risk," is unaffected by any new investment and financing decision, the capitalization rate is dependent on the financial risk induced by the debt-to-equity ratio or the financing mix adopted by the firm. In that case ρ is specified as $\rho = \rho(K, D)$, where K is the amount of equity capital in the firm, measured at book or balance sheet value, and D refers to the accompanying amount of debt capital. The market value of the debt capital will equal its book value by virtue of the assumptions to be made regarding the roll-over or continual refinancing of maturing debt.

The operating income of the firm can be described as $N = R - C$, where R, gross revenue, will be given by $p(Q)$, the selling price of the firm's output functionally dependent on the quantity of output being sold, times $f(X)$, where $f(X)$ describes the production function of the firm in vector notation, X describing an n-element factor input vector. Operating costs, C, will be similarly defined as $C = a'X$, where the factor cost price vector, a, is, for purposes of simplifying the argument, taken as given. The residual equity earnings before tax are derived from the operating income by deducting the firm's interest burden on its debt capital. This is describable as $r(K, D)D$, or as the average interest rate on debt capital, r, shown also as functionally dependent on the K and D financing mix, multiplied by the amount of debt capital actually being used in the firm. It follows that the maximand function may be written as

$$V = \frac{1}{\rho(K, D)} \left[p(Q)f(X) - a'X - r(K, D)D \right] (1 - t). \qquad (1)$$

The firm's optimization decision process over its $n + 2$ decision variables X_i, K, D must be seen as subject to what we have termed its money capital availability constraint. If a vector of "money capital requirements coefficients," b, is specified, the firm's total money capital requirements can be described as $b'X$, again adopting suitable vector notation. The ith element of the b vector here indicates the number of dollars of money capital that must be invested in the firm (and thereby appear on the assets side of the balance sheet) for each unit of the ith factor capacity employed in the firm.[20] It is this money capital requirements vector that embeds the financing decision and

[20]The questions of the specification of the elements of the a and b vectors and their dependence on the money capital intensity of the various technological factor capacities employed in the firm were examined fully in my *Theory of the Firm*. See there also the discussion of the "effective marginal cost" of the factors or the sum of a "marginal direct cost" and a "marginal imputed money capital cost," in the determination of which the "money capital intensity" of the factor is relevant and the marginal productivity of money capital emerges as the imputation rate.

the firm's relation with the financial markets in its factor employment decision and its technological choice of operating structures. The money capital availability constraint then assumes the form

$$b'X \leq K + D. \tag{2}$$

The firm's constrained objective function for structural planning purposes may be stated as

$$\underset{X_i, K, D}{Max}\ \phi = \frac{1}{\rho(K, D)} [p(Q)f(X) - a'X - r(K, D)\, D]\,(1 - t) + \mu[K + D - b'X] \tag{3}$$

by incorporating (2) in (1). The coefficient on the constraint condition, μ, can be interpreted as the marginal value-productivity of money capital. In this formulation of the problem we are assuming that the firm's money capital availability constraint is operative and that the firm therefore does not enjoy conditions of "money capital saturation." If the firm did enjoy money capital saturation, the solution value of μ would be zero, money capital could not then be said to have an effective marginal opportunity cost, and the "marginal imputed money capital costs" of the various factors employed would also be zero. In such a case we would be back in the simplest neoclassical world. By assuming an operative money capital availability constraint, moreover, the general Kuhn-Tucker form of the structural planning problem reduces to the simpler Lagrange expression in Equation (3).

My interest at present is not in the complete set of extremum conditions implicit in Equation (3), or in working out the interdependent structural planning optima. Consider the following disequilibrium situation. The firm, it is supposed, has available to it a given and fixed amount of equity capital, K, and is considering the economic worthwhileness of introducing a marginal dose of debt capital to the firm. What, then, is to be understood as the "cost" of that debt capital? Or what is the minimum required rate of return which must be earned on investing that marginal debt capital in the firm in order to prevent any dilution of the equity owners' economic wealth position? We begin by partially differentiating the constrained objective function with respect to D.

$$\frac{\partial \phi}{\partial D} = -\frac{\pi(1 - t)}{\rho^2}\frac{\partial \rho}{\partial D} - \frac{1}{\rho}\left[r + \frac{D\,\partial r}{\partial D}\right](1 - t) + \mu = 0. \tag{4}$$

It follows from Equation (4) that

$$\left[r + \frac{D\,\partial r}{\partial D}\right](1 - t) + \frac{V\,\partial \rho}{\partial D} = \rho\mu. \tag{5}$$

Dividing throughout by (1 − *t*) *yields*

$$r + \frac{D\,\partial r}{\partial D} + \frac{V\,\partial \rho}{\partial D} \left[\frac{1}{1-t}\right] = \rho\mu', \tag{6}$$

where μ' equals the marginal productivity measure multiplied by a tax step-up factor to express it on a before-tax basis. The tax step-up factor, which also appears on the left-hand side of the equation, is equal to the reciprocal of one minus the firm's tax rate.

Both sides of the optimization condition in Equation (6) are expressing the firm's marginal cost of debt capital, and the left-hand side exhibits in more detail the "full marginal cost of relaxing the money capital availability constraint." The first two terms taken together describe the derivative of the firm's interest burden with respect to debt, $d[r(K, D)D]/dD$, or the increase in the interest burden that will result from the increased use of debt. We can refer to this magnitude, $(r + D\,\partial r/\partial D)$, as the firm's marginal direct cost of debt. Recognizing the first term, r, as the interest rate which has to be paid on the marginal debt itself, it follows that the marginal direct cost of debt will be greater than the interest cost of the marginal debt. This follows because the increase hereby occurring in the debt-to-equity financing ratio in the firm will imply that the new higher interest rate on debt capital will have to be paid, not only on the new debt now being issued, but also on the amount of the previously existing debt when that matures and has to be refinanced.

But if the newly acquired money capital were to earn simply a rate of return sufficient to cover the marginal direct cost of debt, there would occur a dilution of the equity owners' economic position, thus rendering the proposed investment and financing nonviable. Consider the final derivative on the left-hand side of Equation (6), $\partial\rho/\partial D$. If, again, we make the not unreasonable assumption or risk aversion on the supply side of the equity capital market, the sign on $\partial\rho/\partial D$ can be expected to be positive, and the increased debt-to-equity financing ratio will increase the owners' required rate of return. If there is no offsetting increase in the residual equity earnings, a reduction in the equity valuation of the firm must occur. In order to make the employment of the marginal debt capital worthwhile, therefore, the new investment must generate an earnings stream sufficiently greater than the marginal direct cost of the debt to enable the residual earnings to be increased in turn by a critically specifiable amount. This further incremental earnings stream must be large enough to increase the residual earnings to such an extent that when the new higher equity earnings are capitalized at the new higher capitalization rate the value of the equity will be at least as high as it was before the new investment and financing occurred.

In the interest of concreteness, consider the following example. The magnitudes are hypothetical and no doubt exaggerated, but they exhibit the nature of the causation involved. They reveal also the dangers in relying, in the disequilibrium decision situations actually confronted in the real world, on generalized security market equilibrium data or on weighted average capital cost concepts. Employing a time subscript zero to refer to the firm's situation before the new financing and investment, and subscript one to refer to the situation after the new financing, let us assume the following situation.

D_0 = \$3 million
V_0 = \$6 million
$W_0 = D_0 + V_0$ = \$9 million
$r_0 = 0.05$, DI_0 (Debt Interest) = \$150,000
$\rho_0 = 0.10$
Number of equity shares outstanding = 100,000
Earnings per share (EPS_0) = \$6
Market value per share (S_0) = \$6/.10 = \$60
Marginal debt financing (ΔD) = \$2 million
$r_1 = 0.06$, DI_1 = \$300,000 (after refinancing of all maturing debt)
$\rho_1 = 0.125$
$t_0 = t_1 = 0.50$.

In this situation the full marginal cost of debt in Equation (6) quantifies as follows:

$$r + \frac{D\,\partial r}{\partial D} + \frac{V\,\partial \rho}{\partial D}\left[\frac{1}{1-t}\right] = 0.06$$

$$+ \frac{3(0.01)}{2} + \frac{6(0.025)}{2}\left[\frac{1}{1-0.50}\right] = 0.06$$

$$+ 0.015 + 0.15 = 0.225 \tag{7}$$

Thus in the case in hand the full marginal cost of debt, or the required rate of return on a before-tax basis necessary to establish economic viability, is 22.5 percent. To reinforce the understanding of the relationships involved, consider the following *pro-forma* income statement of the firm.

The relationships envisaged imply that the residual earnings per share of equity after tax would have been increased by \$1.50, sufficient to increase earnings per share to \$7.50. When this amount is capitalized at the new higher capitalization rate of 12.5 percent, the market value per share of \$60 can be maintained and no equity dilution has resulted from the new investment and financing. But this will occur only if the operating income of the firm increased by \$450,000, or by 22.5 percent of the new \$2 million investment, precisely the

Income Statement Data

	Before new Financing	*Required Position after new Financing*	*Incremental data*
	$'000	$'000	$'000
Operating Income	1,350	1,800	450
Less Debt Interest	150	300	150
Earnings before tax	1,200	1,500	300
Less Tax	600	750	150
Net Income (Residual equity earnings)	600	750	150
Earnings per share	$6	$7.5	
Market value per share	$\frac{6}{0.10} = 60$	$\frac{7.5}{0.125} = 60$	—

gross before-tax required rate of return or the full marginal cost of the debt as specified in Equation (7).

In this case, then, the operative cost of capital is 22.5 percent. This is the fully specified decision criterion for investment decision making and is the hurdle rate or the capital budgeting cutoff point for investment expenditure. Though the figures are hypothetical, they disclose the logic of the fact that the 22.5 percent required rate of return on the marginal investment exceeds both the old and the new interest rate on debt capital; it exceeds the old equity capitalization rate multiplied by the tax step-up factor to express it on a before-tax basis; and it is only fractionally lower than the new equity capitalization rate when the latter is similarly raised to its before-tax equivalent. It follows that the operative cost of capital is greater than the weighted average cost of capital, and that if the latter were used as an investment decision criterion, equity value dilution would occur. Taking the before-financing magnitudes, the weighted average cost of capital on a before-tax basis would be

$$\frac{1}{3}\, r_0 + \frac{2}{3}\, \rho_0 \left[\frac{1}{1-t}\right] = 0.05/3 + 0.40/3 = 0.150.$$

Or employing the after-financing magnitudes the weighted average cost of capital quantifies as

$$\frac{5}{11}\, r_1 + \frac{6}{11}\, \rho_1 \left[\frac{1}{1-t}\right] = (0.06)5/11 + (0.125)(2)6/11 = 0.163.$$

There remains a further aspect of the relation between the full marginal cost of debt capital and the full marginal cost of equity. In the same way as the full marginal cost of debt is specified on the left-hand side of Equation (6), the corresponding full marginal cost of equity, obtainable by differentiating the constrained objective function with respect to K, the firm's equity capital decision variable, can be specified as

$$\rho\left[\frac{1}{1-t}\right]+\frac{D\partial r}{\partial K}+\frac{V\,\partial\rho}{\partial K}\left[\frac{1}{1-t}\right]=\rho\mu'.^{21} \qquad (8)$$

In the same way as the assumption of risk aversion on the part of the suppliers of money capital yielded positive signs on the two partial derivatives on the left-hand side of Equation (6), the same assumption yields negative signs on the partials on the left-hand side of Equation (8). An increase in equity capital or a decrease in the debt-to-equity ratio implies a decrease in risk exposure and can be expected to lead to a lower interest rate on debt and a lower capitalization rate on equity.

If the full set of first-order extremum conditions implicit in Equation (3) were specified, then at the extremum condition or the financing mix that provided the minimum attainable weighted average cost of capital it could be shown that the full marginal costs described on the left-hand sides of Equations (6) and (8) are equal to each other and are both equal to the weighted average cost of capital, i, expressed on a before-tax basis as

$$i=r\left[\frac{D}{D+V}\right]+\rho\left[\frac{V}{D+V}\right]\cdot\left[\frac{1}{1-t}\right]=\rho\mu'. \qquad (9)$$

But in reality the actual decision postures we have in view are not such fully generalized equilibrium situations at all. We can note, however, if we bring together Equations (6), (8), and (9), that at fully generalized equilibrium the following relationship holds (recalling again the signs on the partials in the equations)

[21]This result is obtained by setting the partial derivative of Equation (3) with respect to K equal to unity. This is the appropriate extremum condition, specifying that at the optimum situation the last added dollar of equity capital will have added precisely one dollar to the value of the equity owners' interest in the firm. The condition follows from our adopting $V = \pi(1 - t)/\rho$ as our maximand function. If, instead, we had worked consistently with the *net* economic value of the ownership, $V - K$, as our maximand, no changes would have been introduced to the results, but in that case Equation (8) would have followed from setting $\partial(V - K)/\partial K = 0$, a perhaps more familiar form of the extremum condition.

$$r < \rho \left[\frac{1}{1-t}\right] \mu = i < \rho \left[\frac{1}{1-t}\right].^{22} \tag{10}$$

Or, dividing throughout the right-hand portion of this relationship,

$$\mu = \frac{i(1-t)}{\rho} < 1. \tag{11}$$

At the mutually determined optimum structure of the firm, the final solution value of the constraint coefficient, μ, will be less than unity. The extent to which it will fall below unity is influenced by the firm's tax rate, which lowers the effective cost of debt relative to that of equity and accordingly permits marginal investments at lower levels of marginal productivity in view of the tax savings that interest deductibility involves.

For these reasons it is not possible to specify *a priori* the optimum solution value of this marginal productivity variable in any given situation. In the hypothetical case we used in this example the relationship stood as follows:

$$\rho \left[\frac{1}{1-t}\right] \mu = 0.25\mu = 0.225, \tag{12}$$

which implied a solution value of μ of 0.9 on a net after-tax basis or 1.8 on a before-tax basis. The basic desideratum of new investment and financing (namely the avoidance of any dilution of the equity owners' position) will be satisfied only if the marginal productivity conditions give promise that the increments in the income stream made necessary by the induced changes in required rates of return could be realized.

It could be asked, no doubt, why the firm in the particular disequilibrium situation we envisaged should not consider introducing marginal equity capital rather than the debt capital proposed in the example. Because of the different induced effects on the capitalization rates, the marginal cost of equity may actually be lower than that of debt. But the direct comparison of these marginal costs in the actual disequilibrium conditions in which decisions have to be made may not be the only, or the principal, point at issue. Perfectly good but

[22]From Equation (6) the assumedly positive signs on the partial derivatives which result from the assumption of consistent risk-aversion on the part of the suppliers of money capital imply $r < \rho\mu'$. Recalling that $\mu' = \mu/(1-t)$ yields the inequality on the left-hand side of Equation (10). The equality in this expression follows directly from Equation (9), a result established in my *Journal of Finance*, March 1970, article cited, and the right-hand inequality in (10) follows from Equation (8), noting in this case that the assumption of consistent risk-aversion yields negative signs (increased equity implying a reduced debt-equity ratio and lower risk) on the partial derivatives in the equation.

nonfinancial reasons may exist why debt rather than equity financing may be preferred, considerations of control of the firm, for example, and other questions that need not be explored at this time.

Uncertainty and Probability

In the light of the foregoing argument and the concern throughout this book with the interdependence between uncertainty, historic time, and disequilibrium, it will be useful to look briefly, in concluding this Part, at the point that crystallizes our basic dissent from alternative approaches to our area of analysis. The point at issue, the question of sustainable relations between uncertainty and probability, is relevant to decision postures in both the business firm and the financial markets. In Parts II and III I will consider more fully the reasons why the concept and thought forms of probability are not in fact applicable to a large number of economic decisions. These reasons inhere, it will be seen, in an epistemological confusion as to what precisely is being said or claimed in a statement of probability. Remarks at this stage will be confined to only two points.[23]

The first point is grammatical or semantic. Consider a statement of the form: "The probability that an experiment of a designatable type *M* will result in an event of type *N* is such and such. . . ." This *appears to be* a statement about *a particular case* of an experiment of the type indicated. But on deeper analysis the meaning is quite different from what is superficially indicated by its grammatical form, for it is in fact not a statement about a *particular instance* of the envisaged experiment, but about a specifiable *class* of such experiments. Care must be taken, therefore, in applying the notions of probability to real-world business situations when too easy a reliance is being placed on mere grammatical form as distinct from logical substance. Most notably, confusion entering from this source affects the permissible economic interpretation of real-world business investment, the mainspring and

[23]Cf. the brilliant discussion of related issues in Shackle, *Decision, Order, and Time*, Part II, and, for a frequently acute discussion of the related epistemological postures of economics, Martin Hollis and Edward J. Nell, *Rational Economic Man, A Philosophical Critique of Neo-classical Economics* (Cambridge: Cambridge Univ. Press, 1975), pp. 75-79 and passim. See also the recent and important work by Brian J. Loasby, *Choice, Complexity and Ignorance* (Cambridge: Cambridge Univ. Press, 1976) for an insightful discussion of the question of, and grounds for, business decision making. The issues involved have been grasped by Sidney Weintraub who refers in his *Modern Economic Thought* to "Shackle's . . . understanding of the operations of an economy in which anticipations dominate conduct, in which the expectations have an elusive vagueness, an unsureness, and thus an uncertainty in decision-making that escapes model-builders, who graft ill-fitting mathematical probability concepts onto essentially unique and non-repetitive events," p. 4.

sustaining engine of the capitalist process itself. For this reason I have referred consistently to the *uniqueness* of the investment decision, and I have treated at some length the notion of the decision maker's solitary standing in the solitary moment in time, in a uniquely determinable inheritance and confronting a unique decision nexus.[24]

The confusion enters from a failure to distinguish the question: "what will be the result of this or that *particular instance* of an experiment or a performance" from the question: "in what proportions will *one thousand instances* of the *same* experiment or performance, taken as a whole, yield this or that or some other result?"[25] It is necessary to acknowledge that the assignment of a probability distribution to outcomes is in a critical sense an assumption of knowledge. It is an assumption that the structure of reality is such that it can be certainly stated that if an experiment is performed repeatedly, such and such an outcome will emerge in a certain proportion of the total number of outcomes. This assumption of relative frequencies is an assumption of knowledge, and knowledge, we have seen, is the antithesis of uncertainty. Knowledge and uncertainty are mutually exclusive. Uncertainty has to do with the *absence* of knowledge, and, indeed, with the intrinsically unknowable. For knowledge cannot be known before its time.

Quite apart, then, from the solitariness and uniqueness of the decision moment in time, and quite apart from the reasons why the "inheritance" and the delimitable potential of the decision moment cannot be captured again once it is past, it is important to be clear as to the kinds of conditions that must be satisfied in order to render probabilistic argument usable and epistemologically efficient in economics. We can envisage in this respect the differing notions of *a priori* probabilities on the one hand and *statistical* probabilities on the other.

The first envisages the distribution of outcomes generated by "the behavior of a system whose structure we can inspect, and from which we can deduce the relative frequency with which this answer or that will . . . occur when the question, in a form applicable to *any* occasion, is repeatedly asked on one occasion after another."[26] In such a case the outcome variable may legitimately be probabilistically defined, and we may treat our experiment situation in terms of what we have called "distributional variable" outcomes.

The same experiment procedure and interpretation may be adopted when "we may repeatedly observe the behavior of the system in practice and record the frequency with which it gives this or that answer to

[24]Cf. the perceptive observations in Coddington, "Creaking Semaphores," p. 161.
[25]Cf. Shackle, *Decision, Order, and Time*, p. 50.
[26]Ibid., p. 53.

the generalized question."[27] The relative frequencies thus obtained by repeated trials may be referred to as *statistical* probabilities.

Unfortunately, however, the very nature of decision situations in real-world business life, particularly in relation to financial decisions, are most decidedly *not* the kind that permit the inspection of a stable structural system and the assignment of unarguably reliable *a priori* probabilities. The question then becomes one of the extent to which reliance can be placed on the legitimate meaning content and usefulness of *statistical* probabilities in business situations. No doubt such situations do arise, in connection with life insurance company mortality tables for example, but in such a case clarity should be preserved as to the kind of question that is being asked. It is not a question regarding an outcome of a *particular instance*. It is one regarding the *proportions* of outcomes of a certain kind in a *large number* of instances.

Certain conditions must clearly exist, therefore, to permit us to use a distributional variable technique in the handling of uncertainty in actual economic practice. For this to be possible, the issue being brought to question, or the hypothesis being subjected to experiment, must be in a genuine and meaningful sense repetitive or capable of replication, and the assumption must therefore be necessarily imposed upon us by the structure of things that *all possible* outcomes can be *exhaustively* listed and classified quantitatively without residue. This, it would seem, is a tall order in the economic-financial world, and beyond any doubt it points us in the direction of the *uniqueness* of decision situations. It points also to the need to use for our purposes not a *distributional* or a probabilistically interpretable variable at all, but a *nondistributional* variable. I shall deal, in other words, not with *probability* at all, but with a new understanding and interpretation of *possibility*.

It may be rejoined that although in business and financial decision making it is not possible to invoke probability in either an *a priori* or a relative frequency statistical sense, it is nevertheless valid to employ probability in a *subjective* sense and to work with "subjectively assigned," or "as if," probability distributions. This suggestion, however, is quite beside the point, and it fails to understand the meaning of the irreducible uncertainty with which decision making, as we are concerned with it, is confronted. For when the decision situation in view is unique, nonrepetitive, and nonreplicable, then the various possible "hypotheses regarding its outcome are . . . *rivals*, denying and excluding each other."[28] And in such a case, in decision situations

[27]Ibid.
[28]Ibid., p. 60.

that can never be repeated, no meaning attaches to averaging, in, say, a mathematical expectational sense, the values of such rival outcomes.

Probability, it is true, can confer actuarial *knowledge* in appropriately defined contexts. But knowledge of this kind in no sense makes probability suited to the handling of *uncertainty* situations where knowledge is truly beyond our grasp. We have said in a previous context that decisions in the economic-financial world are in the general case *self-destructive* decisions, meaning by this that the making of them destroys beyond recapture the decision nexus that once existed and which gave rise to them.

II

Equilibrium Theory of Financial Asset Prices: Theory, Application, Critique

4

Utility, Probability, and a Separation Theorem

In this and the following chapters of Part II I set out the essential components and conclusions of the equilibrium theory of financial asset prices. The argument, however, will be confined to exhibiting the *essential structure* of the equilibrium theory, and I shall establish the usual assumption content and the principal conclusions extruded from it. But I will not have occasion in the space available to consider many of the changes and modifications of assumptions that might be introduced to the theory, the attempts that have thereby been made to bring it into closer contact with the actual world of affairs, or the "empirical testing" that has been conducted in many directions. The relevant literature abounds in subtle variations on the theoretical theme and on empirical implications.[1] But my objective is not to evaluate or extend the refinements or the superstructure that have been built on the foundations to be examined. Rather, my task is that of a more radical critique of the presuppositions and the logical structure of the theory itself. In this chapter we shall consider some fundamental tools of analysis, and in Chapter 5 I will exhibit the principal conclusion of the theory. The fundamental critique and conclusions as to the reasons why the real-world relevance of the equilibrium theory has seriously to be called in question will then be presented, as a prelude to a consideration in Part III of an alternative line of theoretical analysis.

It will be necessary for present purposes to exposit a number of theoretical conceptions and tools of analysis from which I shall subsequently dissent. But the construction of them at this stage is a neces-

[1]See Jensen, *Studies in Capital Markets*, notably Parts II and III on empirical findings and extensions of the theory, and the same author's "Capital Markets: Theory and Evidence," *The Bell Journal of Economics and Management Science* (Autumn, 1972). See also Mossin, *Theory of Financial Markets*, Haley and Schall, *The Theory of Financial Decisions*, Fama and Miller, *Theory of Finance*, and Hirshleifer, *Investment, Interest, and Capital*.

sary prelude to the clearer apprehension of the reorganization of the theory I have in view. Under this heading I have in mind the notions of utility, probability, the fixedness of time horizons in portfolio selection and asset choice theory, and the locking in of the analysis to comparative equilibria, to the neglect of an analysis of the motion and change and the speculative exploitation of events in historic time.

It is necessary to take account also of the pervasive phenomenon of "false trading," both in the financial markets and in the real markets of the economy that are interconnected with them. The phenomenon and effects of false trading strike most damagingly at the heart of the static, timeless, equilibrium theory.[2] But initially, we shall assume, in the same way as Fama and Miller, for example, have made explicit, that transactions in the financial asset market are consummated only at "equilibrium" or "market clearing" prices, or that "equilibrium is reached through a process of tatonnement with recontracting."[3] Then in our final critique of the conventional analysis, which turns substantially on the asset portfolio choice theory of Markowitz, Tobin, Hicks and others, these restrictive assumptions will be replaced by an alternative viewpoint.[4]

Subjectively Assigned Probability

The investment attractiveness of an individual asset is assumed by the equilibrium pricing theory to be dependent on the expected return it offers the investor over a designated holding period (say a year) and the degree of risk to which the investor would be exposed during that time by the holding of it. The expected return and risk are defined by the first and second moments of a subjectively assigned probability distribution of the asset's prospective single period return.

We may suppose that the asset is a share of common stock of the jth firm among the population of firms whose securities are listed on the New York Stock Exchange. Then the single period return on that asset, R_{jt}, during the holding period t, may be defined as

$$\tilde{R}_{jt} = (\tilde{D}_{jt} + \tilde{P}_{jt} - P_{jt-1})/P_{jt-1}, \tag{1}$$

where D_{jt} equals the dividend paid on the stock during the period, and the time-subscripted P_j terms refer to the market value of the stock at

[2]Cf. Douglas Vickers, "Finance, and False Trading in Non-tatonnement Markets," *Australian Economic Papers* (December 1975).

[3]Cf. Fama and Miller, *Theory of Finance*, p. 278.

[4]Cf. Markowitz, *Portfolio Selection*, Tobin, "Theory of Portfolio Selection," and the same author's "Liquidity Preference as Behaviour Towards Risk," *Review of Economic Studies* 25 (February 1958), and Hicks, *Critical Essays* chapter 6, "The Pure Theory of Portfolio Selection."

the end of the preceding and the current periods. The tildes on certain of the variables indicate that their values are stochastically defined rather than uniquely specifiable at the beginning of the *t*th period. The return potentially realizable on the asset is in effect made up of two parts: first, the dividend yield deriving from the first term in the numerator of the equation; and second, the capital gain (or loss), or $P_{jt} - P_{jt-1}$.

The R_{jt} is interpretable as a random variable dependent on the stochastic properties of the dividend and terminal price variables. For the purposes in hand, then, R_{jt} is describable by a subjectively assigned probability distribution. The expected return on the asset, $E(\tilde{R}_{jt})$, is definable as the expected value of that probability distribution, and the risk may be defined by the variance of the same distribution, Var $(\tilde{R}_{jt})$. We are imagining, that is to say, that risk is exhaustively conceptualized in terms of the prospective variability of returns.

If, now, the investor were to conceive of the desirability of dividing his investable money capital between two such asset opportunities, his possible return and risk exposure during the contemplated holding period would depend on (1) the same expected value and variance parameters of the probability distributions of return assigned to each of the assets, (2) the degree of correlation between the returns on the respective assets, and (3) the relative proportions of the total portfolio allocated to each of the assets. Notationally, the expected return and the variance of return of a portfolio made up of such assets *A* and *B* could be defined as

$$E(\tilde{R}_P) = w_A E(\tilde{R}_A) + w_B E(\tilde{R}_B) \tag{2}$$

and

$$\text{Var}\,(\tilde{R}_P) = w^2_A \,\text{Var}\,(\tilde{R}_A) + w^2_B \,\text{Var}\,(\tilde{R}_B) + 2w_A w_B \,\text{Cov}\,(\tilde{R}_A, \tilde{R}_B). \tag{3}$$

In this latter expression, the w_A, w_B terms represent the weights allocated to the respective assets in the portfolio, subject to the proviso $w_A + w_B = 1$. The covariance term, Cov $(\tilde{R}_A, \tilde{R}_B)$, can alternatively be written as

$$\text{Cov}\,(\tilde{R}_A, \tilde{R}_B) = \rho_{AB}\sigma_A\sigma_B, \tag{4}$$

taking account of the familiar statistical relation between contemporaneous random variables, where ρ_{AB} refers to the correlation coefficient between the asset random returns and σ_A and σ_B refer to the standard deviations of the probability distributions of the respective asset returns.

Consider the coordinates of the asset *A* and *B* investment opportunities in the risk-return plane in Figure 2. For the present we may ignore the three loci connecting *A* and *B*.

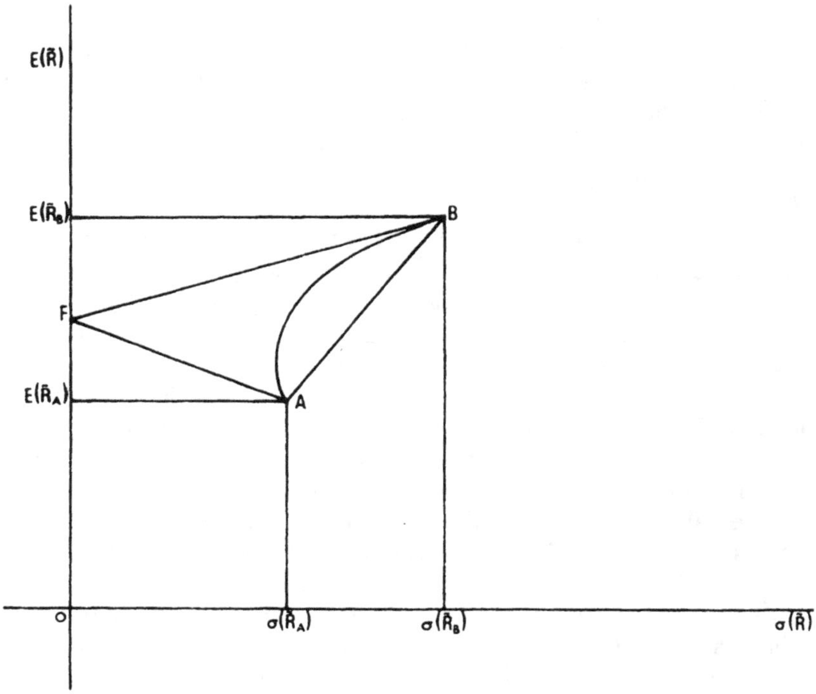

Figure 2.

At this stage we shall drop the tildes from the random variables in the interest of notational economy, and making use of Equation (4) we may rewrite Equation (3) as

$$\text{Var}(R_P) = w_A{}^2 \text{Var}(R_A) + w_B{}^2 \text{Var}(R_B) + 2w_A w_B \rho_{AB} \sigma_A \sigma_B. \quad (5)$$

If, then, the investor were to construct a portfolio of assets A and B whose returns were perfectly correlated, or where $\rho_{AB} = 1$, the standard deviation of the return on the portfolio could be written as

$$\sigma(R_P) = w_A \sigma_A + w_B \sigma_B. \quad (6)$$

The question that now presents itself is how the investor could take advantage of different possible degrees of correlation between asset returns in order to achieve different possible risk-return tradeoffs from alternative portfolio choices and combinations of assets. We may consider this question by looking at the weights, w_A and w_B, which the investor might assign to the respective assets in his portfolio. Writing w_B as $(1 - w_A)$ and differentiating Equation (2) with respect to w_A,

$$\frac{dE(R_P)}{dw_A} = E(R_A) - E(R_B). \tag{7}$$

Similarly, differentiation of Equation (6) implies

$$\frac{d\sigma(R_P)}{dw_A} = \sigma_A - \sigma_B. \tag{8}$$

Dividing Equation (7) by Equation (8),

$$\frac{dE(R_P)}{d\sigma(R_P)} = \frac{E(R_A) - E(R_B)}{\sigma_A - \sigma_B}. \tag{9}$$

This implies that in the simple case in which the asset returns are perfectly positively correlated, the attainable portfolio risk-return tradeoff described in Equation (9) is a linear relation, all terms in this expression being given once the forms (and therefore the first and second moments) of the probability distributions of the asset returns have been specified subjectively by the investor.

This portfolio risk-return tradeoff is depicted in Figure 2 as the easternmost linear locus joining the points A and B. The investor could achieve any desired portfolio expected return between $E(R_A)$ and $E(R_B)$ by varying the weights assigned to the respective assets in his portfolio, thereby exposing himself to varying degrees of risk. If, unlike the case we have just considered of perfectly correlated asset returns where $\rho = 1$, we conceived of correlation values of less than unity, then it would follow that for any combination of assets the portfolio risk for any given level of expected return would be lower as that correlation coefficient was lower. Indeed, as seen from Equation (5), if a combination is made of assets whose returns are *negatively* correlated, the final term in the equation will be negative, and the variance of return on the portfolio will be less than the weighted sum of the variances on the individual assets. Considerations of this kind may then generate the portfolio risk-return tradeoff described by the intermediate curvilinear locus between A and B in Figure 2. A specified level of expected return is then attainable at a lower portfolio risk exposure than would be possible if the asset returns were perfectly correlated. For any specified level of portfolio risk a higher return can be expected.

Consider now the case in which the asset returns are perfectly negatively correlated, or where $\rho = -1$. It then follows from Equation (5) that

$$\sigma(R_P) = w_A\sigma_A - w_B\sigma_B, \tag{10}$$

or, recalling that $w_A + w_B = 1$,

$$\sigma(R_P) = w_A\sigma_A - (1 - w_A)\sigma_B. \tag{11}$$

It follows that for a zero risk portfolio, or for the case in which $\sigma(R_P) = 0$,

$$w_A = \sigma_B/(\sigma_A + \sigma_B). \tag{12}$$

It is then conceptually possible to choose the asset portfolio weights in such a way, specifying w_A as shown in Equation (12), that the overall risk on the portfolio is reduced to zero. This possibility is depicted by the two-segment linear locus in Figure 2, where a risk-free portfolio is envisaged with an expected rate of return indicated by the point F on the vertical axis.

The foregoing argument can be generalized to an n-asset portfolio where n represents any desired number of assets or members of an asset investment opportunity set. Given the subjectively assigned probability distributions of asset returns, and given also the covariance matrix that derives from the correlations between the individual asset returns, the following expressions for portfolio returns and risks can be envisaged:

$$E(R_P) = \sum_{i=1}^{n} w_i E(R_i), \sum w_i = 1 \tag{13}$$

and

$$\sigma^2(R_P) = \sum_{i=1}^{n} w_i{}^2 \sigma^2(R_i) + 2 \sum_{i=1}^{n} \sum_{j>i}^{n} w_i w_j \rho_{ij} \sigma_i \sigma_j \tag{14}$$

or

$$\sigma(R_P) = \left[\sum_i \sum_j w_i w_j \sigma_{ij} \right]^{\frac{1}{2}} \tag{15}$$

where σ_{ij} represents the covariance term if $i \neq j$ and the variance when $i = j$.

If it is decided to add a new asset to an already existing portfolio, the effect on the risk of the portfolio will depend on three things: first, the variance of return of the asset that is being added; second, the redistribution of relative portfolio weights over the various assets, where the proportionate portfolio weights, w_i, must sum to unity; and third, the covariances between the returns on the asset being added and those of each of the previously existing assets in the portfolio.

In the risk-return plane of Figure 3 it follows that if correlations were perfect the linear portfolio loci of AB, BC, or AC could be attained. But the locus ABC would "dominate" that of AC, because portfolio combinations along ABC would offer, for specified degrees or risk, a higher level of expected return. Moreover, assets A and B,

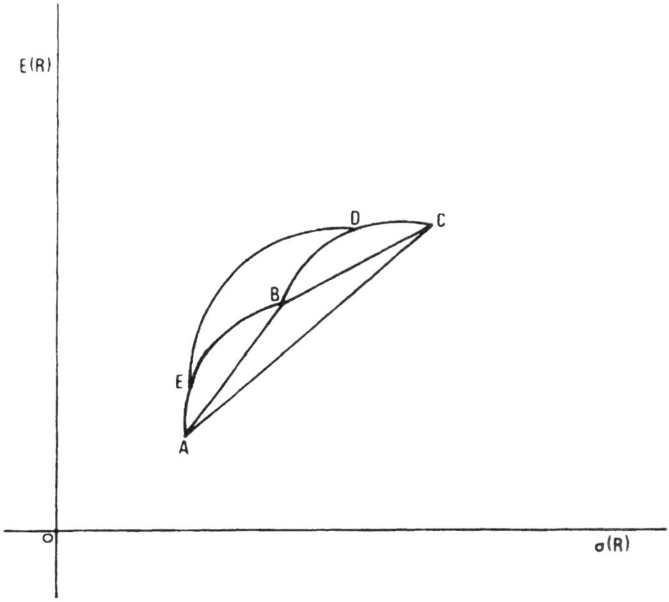

Figure 3.

depending on the correlation between their returns, could be combined in a portfolio to provide a risk-return profile described by point *E*. Similarly, *B* and *C* might be combined to provide a portfolio described by the point *D*. Then portfolios *D* and *E* might in turn be combined, by choosing appropriate asset weights, to provide a further curvilinear opportunity locus which dominates all of those so far mentioned, namely *CDEA*.

In short, the *n*-asset opportunity set can be generalized to provide a nonlinear portfolio locus of the form *EE* indicated in Figure 4. This locus may be referred to as the boundary of the efficient opportunity set or as the locus of efficient asset portfolios. The reason for the nonlinearity of this locus lies in the same phenomena that gave rise to the intermediate curvilinear locus in Figure 2 or those in Figure 3, namely the possibilities of taking advantage of the less than perfect correlations between individual asset returns.

The locus *EE* in Figure 4 is referred to as the efficient portfolio opportunity boundary because every point on this locus dominates attainable portfolios interior to the opportunity set. Every portfolio between *R* and *S*, for example, dominates portfolios in the interior of the segment *RMS* by offering a higher return for a specified degree of risk or a lower degree of risk for a given expected return. In this sense the boundary *EE* can itself be said to be undominated.

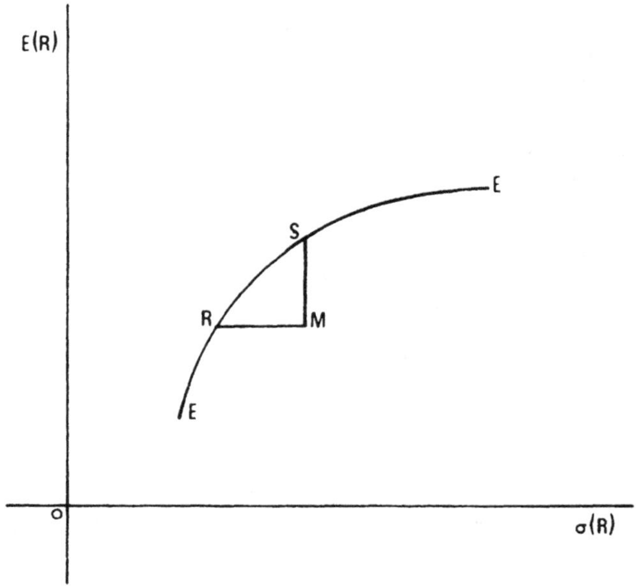

Figure 4.

Given that the efficient locus *EE* is objectively calculable, once we are given the forms of the subjectively assigned probability distributions of the underlying asset returns and the relevant covariance matrix, the *EE* locus can be regarded as the *objectively attainable* asset market risk-return tradeoff. The slope of the locus at any point, $dE(R)/d\sigma(R)$, describes the objectively attainable marginal rate of transformation between risk and return.

Any point on the efficient portfolio locus *EE* is a potential equilibrium point for the investor. The question then arises: which, out of all the potential efficient equilibrium portfolios, will be the one actually selected by an investor? Consistent with the thrust of neoclassical theory, we may bring into juxtaposition with one another the two conceptual measures: first, the *objectively attainable marginal rate of transformation* between risk and return that we have just described; and second, the *subjectively acceptable marginal rate of substitution* between risk and return. We can expect equilibrium optima to be associated with the relation between these two marginal rates.

This will turn out to be the case, but before putting any more of the equilibrium theoretic structure in place we turn to an examination of the related theory of utility.

Utility and Probability

Consider now the investment opportunities and prospects confronting an investor who approaches the financial asset market at the beginning of time period t with a specified total wealth endowment of W_t. In the fuller development of the equilibrium asset theory the notion of *given* wealth endowments plays a very important part; and indeed, in contradiction of such a postulate, the effects on actual wealth endowments, the windfall, spillover, and asset value redistribution effects, will be a significant implication of the false trading that occurs in the real and the financial markets.

Interest can now focus on the potential accumulated value of the investor's wealth at the end of a single time period t if investment were made at an available market rate of return specified as R_t. It follows that

$$\tilde{W}_{t+1} = (1 + \tilde{R}_t)W_t. \tag{16}$$

Again the tildes on R_t and W_{t+1} indicate that the market rate of return during the period is understood as a random variable, and that the wealth value attainable at the end of the period is stochastically described. Our interest centers now in the attractiveness to the investor of his expectations of W_{t+1}. Clearly, we are pointed here in the direction of the neoclassical theory of utility.

Positing a utility function defined over the random variable W, we shall invoke the familiar Neumann-Morgenstern approach to preference orderings over objects of choice, relying on axioms of comparability or pairwise comparison, transitivity, continuity, convexity, and monotonicity to provide "representable" preference orderings and an ordinal utility function representing or reflecting those orderings.[5]

As we are dealing with a utility function defined over a random variable, W, we are interested in the stochastic properties of that variable, or in the moments, principally the expected value and the variance, of the relevant probability distribution.

For concreteness we shall assume a second degree utility function defined over the random rate of return, R_t,

$$U(\tilde{R}) = \alpha\tilde{R} - \beta\tilde{R}^2. \tag{17}$$

[5]The considerable body of material on preference ordering and utility theory that must here be passed over can be inspected in R. Duncan Luce and Howard Raiffa, *Games and Decisions* (New York: Wiley, 1957), chapter 2; J. von Neumann and Oskar Morgenstern, *Theory of Games and Economic Behaviour*, 2d ed. (Princeton: Princeton Univ. Press, 1947); Peter Newman, *The Theory of Exchange* (Englewood Cliffs, N.J.: Prentice-Hall, 1965), chapter 2; Fama and Miller, *Theory of Finance*, chapter 5; and Hirshleifer, *Investment, Interest and Capital*, chapter 8.

For notational economy the tildes will be omitted from the random variables, and we acknowledge that an investor is interested in the *expected utility* which the market prospects before him provide. Taking, therefore, the expected value of Equation (17),

$$E[U(R)] = \alpha E(R) - \beta E(R^2). \tag{18}$$

The second term on the right-hand side of Equation (18), the expectation of the square of the random variable, equals the sum of the square of the mean and the variance of the probability distribution of the variable. This is to say,

$$E(R^2) = [E(R)]^2 + \text{Var}\,(R), \tag{19}$$

or, employing alternative notation,

$$E(R^2) = \mu^2 + \sigma^2. \tag{20}$$

Substituting Equation (20) in Equation (18) yields

$$E(U) = \alpha\mu - \beta\mu^2 - \beta\sigma^2. \tag{21}$$

This last equation is an expression in the moments, the mean and the standard deviation, of the probability distribution of the random rate of return. Thus a *second degree utility function* defined over the random variable R in Equation (17) has been *transformed into an expected utility function* defined over the first *two* moments of the probability distribution of the random variable over which the original utility function was defined.

The original utility function in Equation (17) can be referred to as a "strict risk aversion" function. It reflects a strictly risk-averting attitude on the part of the investor whose preferences it summarizes. The strict risk aversion property is implied in the expected utility function in Equation (21). Focusing on the marginal expected utility of risk, connoted by the dispersion parameter of the probability distribution, and differentiating Equation (21) with respect to this argument provides

$$\frac{d[E(U)]}{d\sigma} = -2\beta\sigma. \tag{22}$$

This indicates that the marginal expected utility of risk is everywhere negative. Similarly, the marginal expected utility of return,

$$\frac{d[E(U)]}{d\mu} = \alpha - 2\beta\mu, \tag{23}$$

is positive for a range of expected returns less than $\alpha/2\beta$. In short, the investor whose attitudes and preferences are captured in the underlying utility function in Equation (17) is attracted by expected return and repelled by risk.

Difficulties inhere in the assumption that all investors' attitudes could always be described by the simple second degree utility function we have employed for purposes of illustration. For it carries the disadvantage of positing a possibly negative marginal utility of expected return at high levels of return in cases where the underlying probability distribution confronting the investor has a high mathematical expectation.

Alternative forms of the utility function can be posited, asymptotic or higher degree functions for example, that circumvent the difficulty we have just acknowledged. But it is beyond our immediate purpose to survey the extensive literature surrounding this issue. We are now equipped with the essential notion of an expected utility function defined over the moments of the probability distribution of the random variable of interest. Concentration on the mean and the variance of such a distribution provides the conceptual foundations of the "mean-variance" approach to decision making under uncertainty. But "uncertainty" in this traditional analysis is used in the sense of what we referred to in the beginning as "probabilistically reducible risk," and not in the sense of genuine residual uncertainty.

Employing this mean-variance approach to the investor's decision problem, it is possible to describe the iso-expected-utility contours in the mean-variance or the risk-return plane implicit in Equation (21), or in the generalized function

$$E(U) = f(\mu, \sigma). \tag{24}$$

These iso-utility contours are shown as indifference curves, analogous with comparable curves from other parts of neoclassical theory, in Figure 5. In this figure the indifference curves represent increasing levels of expected utility as movement is made across the map in the northwesterly direction indicated by the arrow.

The slope of an indifference curve at any specified point denotes the *subjectively acceptable marginal rate of substitution* (MRS) between risk and return. As the curves are drawn in Figure 5 the assumption of a diminishing MRS is reflected in the convexity downwards of the curves. Recalling Mossin's summary statement that decision making under uncertainty deals with "choices among probability distributions," in the case depicted the investor would require increasingly large increments of expected return to compensate him for successive increments of risk, to allow him to remain at a specified level of utility.[6]

[6]Mossin, *Theory of Financial Markets*, p. 6.

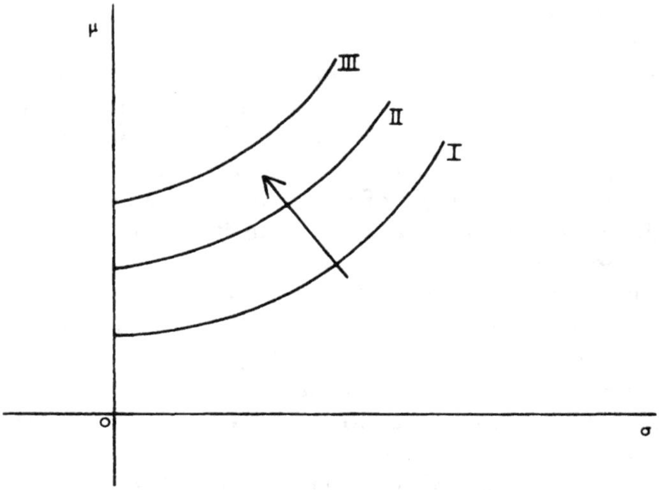

Figure 5.

For concreteness, let us envisage the indifference curve family implicit in the expected utility function of Equation (21). Setting the differential of the function equal to zero for the specification of an iso-utility indifference contour,

$$dE(U) = (\alpha - 2\beta\mu)d\mu - 2\beta\sigma\, d\sigma = 0, \tag{25}$$

whence it follows that

$$\frac{d\mu}{d\sigma} = \frac{2\beta\sigma}{\alpha - 2\beta\mu}. \tag{26}$$

The slope of the indifference curve is thus dependent on the α and β parameters of the original utility function. In the case at hand the slope can be shown to be positive. Downward convexity is confirmed by the positive sign on the second derivative $d^2\mu/d\sigma^2$ obtained by differentiation of Equation (26):

$$\frac{d^2\mu}{d\sigma^2} = \frac{2\beta}{(\alpha - 2\beta\mu)^3}\left[(\alpha - 2\beta\mu)^2 + 4\beta^2\sigma^2\right] > 0 \tag{27}$$

The positivity on this expression is guaranteed by our recognition that in working with a simple second degree utility function we should have to restrict expected return magnitudes to levels such that $\mu < \alpha/2\beta$. This implies $\alpha - 2\beta\mu > 0$, supplying positivity on the denominator in Equation (27). This confirms the investor's diminishing MRS between risk and return.

If the investor's utility function in the random rate of return were, say, of the *third* degree form

$$U(R) = \alpha R - \beta R^2 + \gamma R^3, \tag{28}$$

this could be shown in a manner analogous with the foregoing to be transformable into an *expected* utility function defined over the first *three* moments of the probability distribution of the underlying random variable. It follows that a utility function of the nth degree in a random variable can be similarly transformed into an expected utility function defined over the first n moments of the underlying probability distribution of the random variable.

In the third degree case, the intrusion into the expected utility function of the third moment, or the measure of skewness, of the distribution of possible returns would indicate that positive skewness was attractive to the investor. The investor would then be taking a favorable attitude to higher expected returns, would be unfavorably disposed to variability of returns, and would be favorably impressed by the possibility, even if small, of higher returns as indicated by a positive skewness of the probability distribution.

It might appear now that the theory of the demand for financial assets and therefore of financial asset prices could be terminated by marrying the investor's subjectively determined family of indifference curves in Figure 5 with the objectively attainable opportunity locus of Figure 4. In that case a point of tangency between the opportunity locus, and an indifference curve would imply that the investor had chosen an efficient portfolio such that (1) he thereby attained his highest possible utility level, and (2) this was confirmed by the fact that his subjectively acceptable MRS between risk and return precisely equalled the objectively attainable marginal rate of transformation between risk and return.

But such a conclusion would be premature. Resolution of the matter must await the acquisition of a little more scaffolding, the erection of which will engage us in the next chapter.

Production-Consumption Separation

At the center of the equilibrium theory of financial asset prices is an important "separation theorem." This demonstrates that the investor's decision as to the optimum structure of his *risky* asset portfolio can be *separated from* his decision as to the proportion of his total wealth endowment he should place in this risky portfolio on the one hand, and the proportion he should hold in a highly liquid or risk-free asset on the other. Comparable considerations arise in the theory of the firm, in the form of whether its investment decision can be separated from its decision regarding its optimum mix of financing sources, and whether its production and factor employment decision can be separated from its investment and financing decisions.

It will place these questions in perspective to consider the following highly abbreviated separation theoretic analysis. Consider for this purpose an individual who (1) possesses a given resource endowment at the present time, t_0, and who has the sure prospect of a further income endowment accruing at the end of one time period from the present, at t_1; (2) is confronted with definable intertemporal production opportunities extending over the same single time period; and (3) has the opportunity of borrowing or lending over the same time period at a given and exogenously determined market rate of interest. Such a situation is described in Figure 6.

In Figure 6 the axes labeled t_0 and t_1 respectively are taken to represent resource availabilities at each of the two time dates. The point E indicates that the hypothesized individual's time vector of endowments is described by R_0 and R_1. Through the endowment point

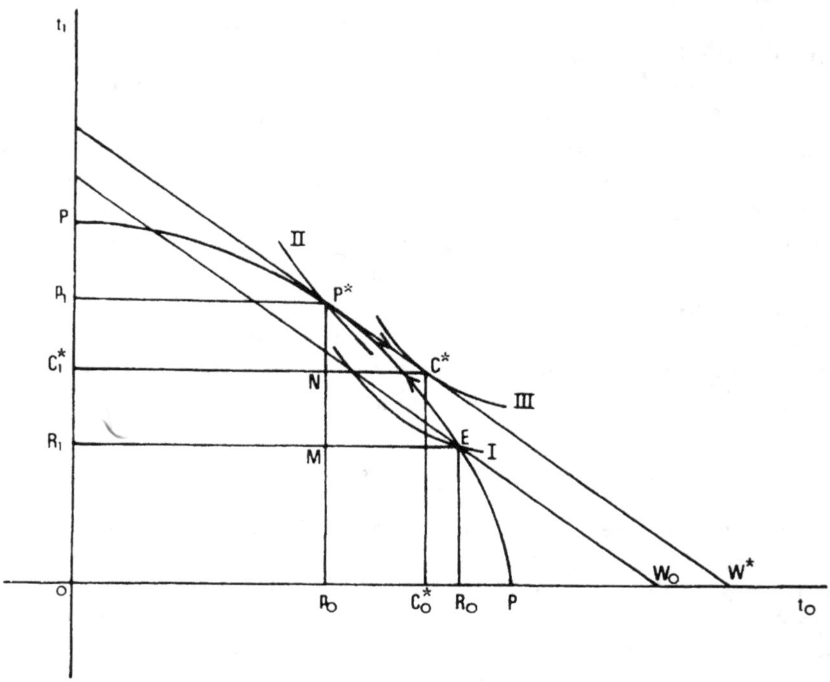

Figure 6.

an intertemporal production possibility or product transformation function, *PP*, is described. This indicates that by consuming less than his given endowment in the current period and devoting part of his resources to production, a larger amount of consumable resources could be made available to the individual in the following period. Clearly, the extent to which it would be economically advisable for him to do this would depend on his intertemporal consumption preferences, on the intertemporal production possibilities, and, as we shall see, on the externally given market rate of interest.

Let us assume that the market rate of interest, r, is implicitly defined by the slope of the valuation line intercepting the t_0 axis at W_0. The magnitude W_0 then describes the value of the individual's endowment vector, measured in present value magnitudes, by virtue of its passing through endowment point E. In other words,

$$W_0 = R_0 + R_1/(1 + r), \tag{29}$$

and every point on the same valuation line would have the same present value.

An indifference curve through the endowment point E, labeled I, indicates that in light of the intertemporal production possibilities, E does not lie on the highest attainable indifference curve. For by moving along the production transformation function from E in the direction indicated by the arrow the individual can climb on to higher indifference curves. He would then be investing part of his currently available resources in production activities, the output of which would accrue in the following period.

The extent of such an intertemporal resource reallocation will depend on the given rate of interest. For the production possibility function is crossing a family of valuation lines, which are parallel by virtue of the given rate of interest, and the optimum production point will be P^* in the diagram. Two conclusions may then be drawn: first, the marginal rate of intertemporal product transformation, or the marginal internal rate of return on resources devoted to production, is equal to the market rate of interest; and second, the individual has maximized his attainable wealth, measured by W^* on the t_0 axis, by reason of his having climbed on to the highest attainable valuation line.

The individual would then realize a product vector (p_0, p_1) which would imply the investment of current resources of $EM = R_0p_0$ in exchange for future resources $MP^* = R_1p_1$. But the vector (p_0, p_1), even though it implies a maximum attainable wealth position W^*, will still not represent the individual's optimum intertemporal consumption allocation.

Consider now the indifference curve, labeled II, which cuts the production function and the valuation line at P^*. The individual can attain a higher level of utility by moving back along the highest attainable valuation line in the direction of the arrow. In Figure 6 he will move to the optimum consumption point C^*, at which an indifference curve is tangential to the valuation line. At such point the marginal rate of intertemporal resource substitution in consumption will be equal to the market rate of interest, and also, therefore, equal to the marginal rate of intertemporal resource transformation in production.

By taking these actions our individual has made two moves which, by virtue of the *given* market rate of interest, we can regard as *separable*. That is to say, the *separation theorem* holds that the optimum intertemporal consumption decision is *separable from* the corresponding production decision. The individual can thus be thought of as moving first from his endowment point E to the optimum production point P^*, and then back to the optimum consumption point C^*. But in making the move from P^* to C^* the individual has *borrowed*, at the market rate of interest, an amount of consumable resources equal to C^*N in present value terms, and he will therefore have to repay this amount out of the next period's production, an amount equal to P^*N in next period values. It is this borrowing and subsequent repayment, undertaken in order to maximize utility, that transmutes the production vector (p_0, p_1) into the consumption vector (C_0^*, C_1^*).

Alternatively, by comparing the original endowment point E and the final optimum consumption point C^* we could regard the overall operation as reducing the current consumption from the current endowment of R_0 to C_0^*, the difference between these two amounts being allocated to production. Then a further amount of $C_0^*p_0$ is borrowed and also allocated to production, in order that in the next period the total amount of resources will be increased from the endowment of R_1 to p_0P^*. Out of this latter total the amount of NP^* will be used to repay borrowing, and the residue of $p_0N = OC_1^*$ will be available for consumption.

The Ownership of Firms

A comparable separation theorem relevant to a firm's operations envisages the separation of its investment from its financing decisions. We can consider this more briefly with the aid of Figure 7. The firm itself is assumed to have no initial resource endowment, and its intertemporal production possibility function, OP, therefore emanates from the origin of the diagram. Magnitudes to the right of the origin on the horizontal axis represent individuals' positive resource availabilities measured in present value terms, and magnitudes to the left represent

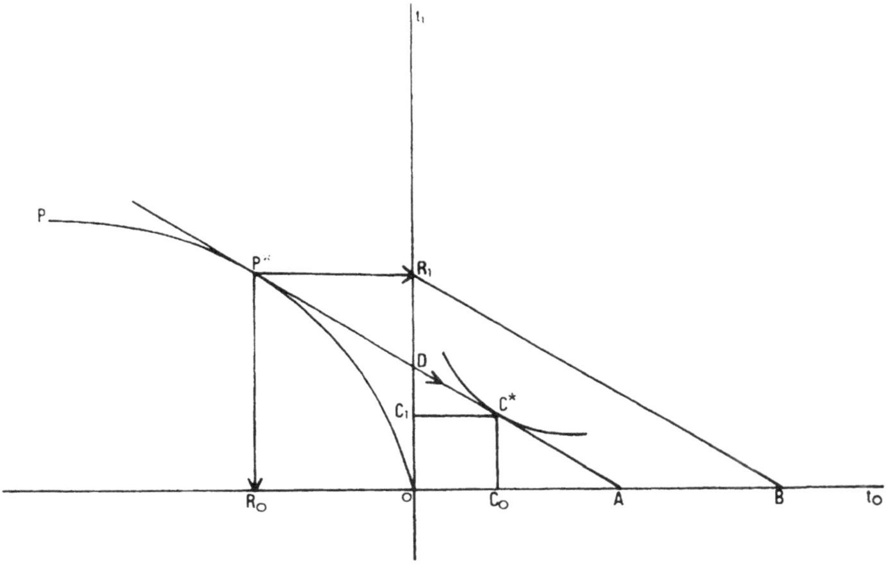

Figure 7.

resource amounts which have been borrowed by firms from individuals and employed as inputs to the production process. As before, valuations are assumed to occur at an externally given market rate of interest, implicit in the slope of the parallel valuation lines P^*A and R_1B.

In the conditions envisaged in Figure 7 the firm will borrow an amount equal to OR_0 in the present period and will use this as an input to production to realize an output of $R_0P^* = OR_1$ in the next period. The optimality of the production point P^* follows from the equality between the marginal rate of resource transformation in production and the market rate of interest. Borrowings equal $OR_0 = R_1P^* = AB$, and the repayment out of the next period's production will equal R_1D. This implies that of the next period's production of OR_1, the net amount remaining to the owners of the firm will be OD. Alternatively, in current value terms the gross output from production equals OB, of which AB is used to repay borrowing and OA remains for the owners.

The owners' consumption opportunity set is described by the triangular space ODA. The owners need not wait until the acquisition of OD resources in the next period before they consume. Given the market rate of interest, they may move down along the valuation line DA until they reach their optimum consumption point C^*. At this point their subjective MRS between present and future consumption is equal to the market rate of interest at which they have borrowed.

The owners, then, will borrow $OC_0 = C_1C^*$ for present consumption, in exchange for which they will repay C_1D out of their future expected net income. The remaining part of this net income, OC_1, will then be available for consumption in the next period.

In this exercise, ***given the market rate of interest***, the firm's investment, production, and financing decision, are ***separable from*** the owners' consumption decisions. The form of the owners' consumption utility function, in other words, is quite irrelevant to the firm's optimal borrowing, investment, and production decisions. Given the market rate of interest, and ***given the ability of both the firm and its individual owners to borrow at that rate***, the only thing the firm's management need worry about is the maximization of the present value of the future revenue stream of the firm. This it accomplishes in the case in hand by investing in order to produce at P^*, while the owners' ability to borrow, at the market rate of interest, or to sell claims against their future expected income, enables them to achieve any intertemporal consumption vector they wish.

Financing Separation in the Firm

From a different viewpoint, we may suppose that the firm's investment expenditure decision for the current period has been made and that the management is concerned only with the manner in which the capital outlay involved should be financed. The firm's revenue inflow in any period is available for (1) paying interest on its outstanding debt and making repayment of maturing debt, (2) paying dividends on the common stock, and (3) financing new investment expenditures. That is to say,

$$R_0 = F_0 + D_0 + I_0 \tag{30}$$

where R, F, D, and I refer respectively to revenue inflow, debt service payments, common stock dividends, and investment expenditures. The subscript again indicates the time period in view.

It follows that dividends could be increased if a larger proportion of the capital expenditure budget were financed by raising debt capital. In the dividend equation,

$$D_0 = R_0 + B_0 - I_0, \tag{31}$$

where B_0 refers to new debt financing, the decision to increase the contribution of B_0 to the capital expenditure budget I_0 could also be regarded as a decision to use additional borrowing to finance dividend payments.

Let us invoke now the assumption that firms and individuals have access to money capital markets in which the rate of interest is given and fixed. Using the same two-period time horizon analysis, the present value of the owners' interest in the firm will be

$$V_0 = D_0 + D_1/(1 + i), \tag{32}$$

where i is the market rate of interest.

Assume now that the firm borrows B_0, to be repaid with interest at rate i in the following period. The common stock dividend in the initial period is as shown in Equation (31), and the final period's dividend will be

$$D_1 = R_1 - (1 + i)B_0. \tag{33}$$

The economic value of the owners' position, therefore, is established by substituting Equation (31) and (33) into Equation (32) to yield

$$V_0 = R_0 + B_0 - I_0 + \frac{R_1 - (1 + i)B_0}{(1 + i)}, \tag{34}$$

which reduces to

$$V_0 = R_0 - I_0 + R_1/(1 + i). \tag{35}$$

The absence of any debt financing term from the final expression in Equation (35) establishes that under the assumptions of the argument the debt financing policy is irrelevant. Economic optimization points consistently in the direction of maximizing present discounted values of income earning opportunities.

The marginal investment decision can be highlighted briefly as follows. Assume on the basis of Equation (35) that the revenue inflow expected to accrue during the next time period would be R_1 if current investment were zero, and that ΔR_1 describes the incremental inflow attributable to the current investment decision. The valuation equation then reduces to

$$V_0 = R_0 - I_0 + \frac{R_1 + \Delta R_1}{1 + i}$$

or

$$V_0 = R_0 + \frac{R_1}{1 + i} + \frac{\Delta R_1}{1 + i} - I_0. \tag{36}$$

The incremental economic value attributed to the new investment expenditures can then be described as

$$\Delta V = \frac{\Delta R_1}{1 + i} - I_0, \tag{37}$$

and this contains within it the optimization investment decision criterion. Differentiating Equation (37) with respect to I_0 yields, for the extremum condition,

$$\frac{d\Delta V}{dI_0} = \frac{1}{1+i} \cdot \frac{d\Delta R}{dI_0} - 1 = 0.$$

It follows that the optimization condition may be written as

$$d\,\Delta R/dI = 1 + i. \tag{38}$$

This implies that investment should properly continue until the marginal revenue generated by the investment equals the marginal cash flow obligations imposed by the new financing arrangements. The centrality of the assumedly given market rate of interest will be clear. We are thereby alerted to the need to give careful attention to the actual conditions that obtain in the financial markets, to the degrees of perfection and certainty existing there, and to the implications of these data for firms' capital raisings and expenditures.

Quite apart from the assumptions of market perfection and unlimited borrowing and lending opportunities at given market rates of interest, the separation theorems have abstracted completely from uncertainty. Moreover, no account has yet been taken of the ways in which the investment of capital in the firm may induce variations in the firm's optimum factor combinations, or in its optimum degree of real capital or labor intensity. To the extent that induced changes of this latter kind do occur, changes in the firm's "operational leverage" will eventuate, changes will be induced in the degree of risk exposure of the purchasers of the firm's capital securities, and it will not be meaningful to rely on the widespread assumption that corporate investment is "scale changing" only. The same considerations raise the possibility also that quasi-monopolistic or monopsonistic conditions may occur on either side of the money capital market. The resultant elasticity of supply of money capital to firms will influence also the firm's optimum financing mix, or its combination of debt and equity capital.

The equilibrium theory of financial asset prices is a purely competitive, static, timeless theory, interested in specifying the *conditions* that would be satisfied *if* the contemplated markets *were* in full generalized equilibrium. It is, in other words, a "pure exchange" theory, and it does not address itself at all to the nature of the *processes* that might lead to "equilibrium," or to what we have seen in the preceding chapters as the movement and change and flux of real economic affairs.[7] As a pure exchange theory the asset market equilibrium

[7]Ibid., p. 64.

analysis assumes that all transactors enter the market with *given* wealth endowments, which are then assumed not to change. At the same time, the probabilistic description of all of the assets in the investment opportunity set is assumed to be given, agreed, and fixed. If, therefore, there should occur induced changes in firms' production factor proportions, in risk exposures, in elasticities of money capital demands and supplies, and in the amounts and the mix of corporate capital securities outstanding, then we could expect also *variations* in *both* the description of the investment opportunity set *and* actual and induced investor wealth endowments. It would then be necessary to develop a theory directed to the explanation of just such phenomena.

The omission of too many of these considerations suggests that scant reason exists for substantial reliance on the separation theorem on which the conventional theory has come to depend.

5

Asset Market Equilibrium Conditions

In this chapter I consider the theory of asset market equilibrium prices on its own ground, against the backdrop of its own most usually adopted assumptions. Given the quantity of financial securities available for pricing in the market, or given a completely specified "asset investment opportunity set," and given also the wealth endowments with which individuals enter the market or "the total amount of money they want to spend," we can now inspect the principal conclusion of the theory.[1] The "general equilibrium model of the pricing and allocation of the *given supply* of securities . . . describe(s) the characteristics of a situation in which investors' combined demand is equal to the supply for every security."[2]

In the application of the theory to corporate financial decisions it is generally assumed that "the market is always near equilibrium" and that "the market will move toward equilibrium if a disequilibrium condition sets in."[3] But this, we might judge, is a rather serious sleight of hand. For it would seem reasonable to expect financial theory to give closer attention to what, if we may adapt a phrase from Sir Dennis Robertson, we might refer to as "asset values on the wing" and not simply "asset values sitting."[4]

The Principal Equilibrium Condition

For purposes of analysis let us suppose that the jth asset in the financial asset market is a share of common stock of the jth firm whose securities are listed on the New York Stock Exchange. What, then, when fully generalized market equilibrium conditions obtain, will be

[1]Jan Mossin, *Security Pricing Theory and Its Implications for Corporate Investment Decisions* (Morristown, N.J.: General Learning Press, 1972), p. 2.

[2]Mossin, *Theory of Financial Markets*, p. 64, our italics.

[3]Bierman and Hass, *Introduction to Managerial Finance* p. 230.

[4]Cf. D. H. Robertson, *Money*, rev. ed. (London: Nisbet, 1948), p. 37.

the market's required rate of return on, or the yield implicit in the equilibrium market price of, that share of common stock? The result can be put in the following form:

$$E(\tilde{R}_j) = R_F + \beta_j[E(\tilde{R}_M) - R_F] \tag{1}$$

where the following notation applies, the tildes again denoting random variables:

$E(\tilde{R}_j)$ = the equilibrium expected or required rate of return on the *j*th "risky" asset.

R_F = a risk-free rate of return at which all transactors in the market are able to borrow and lend.

$E(\tilde{R}_M)$ = the equilibrium rate of return on a "market portfolio," definable as a weighted combination of *all* assets available in the market, where the weight assigned to each asset is defined as the proportion the equilibrium market value of that asset bears to the total market value of all assets in the opportunity set.

β_j = the ratio of (1) the covariance between the *j*th asset's rate of return and the rate of return on the market portfolio, and (2) the variance of the market portfolio's rate of return.

The last mentioned variable, β_j, is commonly referred to as the *j*th firm's "beta coefficient" and can be depicted alternatively as the analogue of the slope coefficient of the empirical relationship shown in Figure 8.

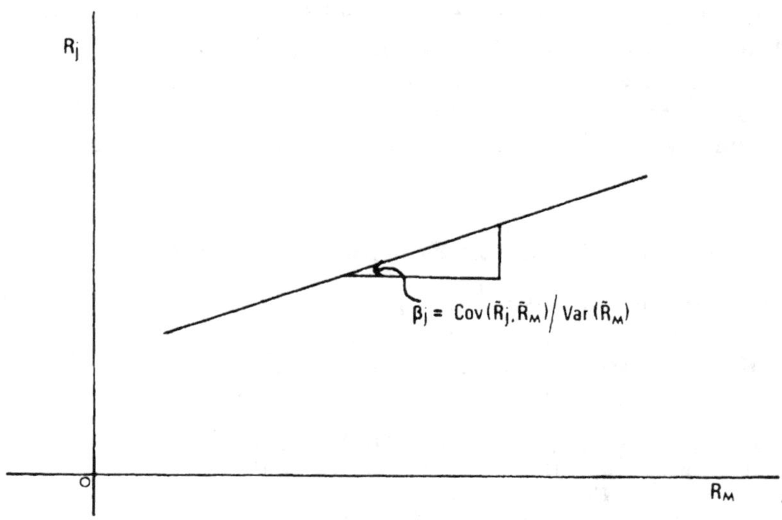

Figure 8.

By substituting the implicit value of the beta coefficient into Equation (1),

$$E(\tilde{R}_j) = R_F + \frac{[E(\tilde{R}_M) - R_F] \operatorname{Cov}(\tilde{R}_j, \tilde{R}_M)}{\operatorname{Var}(\tilde{R}_M)} \tag{2}$$

or

$$E(\tilde{R}_j) = R_F + \lambda \operatorname{Cov}(\tilde{R}_j, \tilde{R}_M), \tag{3}$$

where $\lambda = [E(\tilde{R}_M) - R_F]/\operatorname{Var}(\tilde{R}_M)$ and may be referred to as the "market price of risk."

From Equation (1) it follows that the equilibrium yield on the jth asset is equal to the sum of (1) the risk-free rate and (2) a premium over that rate, the premium being determined by the constant beta coefficient times what can be referred to as the equilibrium market risk premium. Or transposing the first term on the right-hand side of Equation (1), the equilibrium risk premium on the jth asset is equal to a constant times the market risk premium. Alternatively, Equation (3) indicates that the equilibrium yield on the jth asset is a linear function of the covariance between its own rate of return and the return on the market portfolio.

Moreover, the covariance term that appears in Equation (3) is proportional to the marginal impact of the jth asset on the risk of the market portfolio. Measuring the latter by the standard deviation of the market portfolio's rate of return, and taking x_j as the weight that the jth asset has in the market portfolio, it will be shown that

$$\frac{\partial \sigma(\tilde{R}_M)}{\partial x_j} = \frac{\operatorname{Cov}(\tilde{R}_j, \tilde{R}_M)}{\sigma(\tilde{R}_M)}. \tag{4}$$

Using Equation (4), and now referring to $[E(R_M) - R_F]/\sigma(R_M)$ as μ, it follows from substitution in Equation (2) that

$$E(\tilde{R}_j) = R_F + \mu \cdot \partial \sigma(\tilde{R}_M)/\partial x_j \tag{5}$$

That is to say, the equilibrium yield on the jth asset is linearly related to its marginal contribution to the total risk of the total opportunity set of assets. The appropriate measure of *portfolio* risk is the variance of its returns. But the emergence of the *covariance* term as a measure of *individual asset* risk in Equation (3) is a reflection of the fact that whereas most of an asset's own variance will be able to be diversified away by optimum portfolio construction, there will remain a so-called "systematic risk," arising from the asset's covariance with all the other assets in the portfolio. The relation shown in Equation (3) is depicted in Figure 9 as what is widely known as the "Security Market Line."

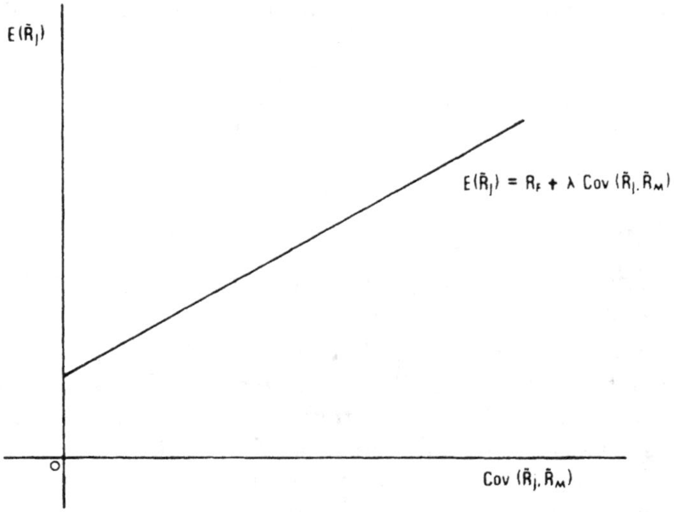

Figure 9.

The foregoing, then, sets before us in Equations (1) and (3) the principal result, or the principal equilibrium condition, of the theory.

The Assumption Content of the Theory

The analysis in the remainder of this chapter will involve the following assumptions.[5]

1. All investors in the financial asset market are single period (all having the same single period time horizon) expected utility of end-of-period wealth maximizers, who choose among alternative portfolios of asset opportunities on the basis of the mean (expected value) and variance of the rate of return. All individuals are optimizing over risk-averse utility functions.

[5]The theory stems principally from the paper by William F. Sharpe, "Capital Asset Prices: A Theory of Market Equilibrium under Conditions of Risk." See also the same author's *Portfolio Theory and Capital Markets* (New York: McGraw-Hill, 1970); Jensen, *Studies in Capital Markets*; Mossin, *Theory of Financial Markets* and "Security Pricing and Investment Criteria in Competitive Markets," *American Economic Review* 59 (December 1969); Eugene F. Fama, "Risk, Return and Equilibrium: Some Clarifying Comments," *Journal of Finance* 23 (March 1968); John Lintner, "The Valuation of Risk Assets and the Selection of Risky Investments in Stock Portfolios and Capital Budgets," *Review of Economics and Statistics* 47 (February 1965), and "Security Prices, Risk and Maximal Gains from Diversification," *Journal of Finance* 20 (December 1965); Haley and Schall, *Theory of Financial Decisions*.

2. All investors can borrow or lend an unlimited amount of funds at an exogenously given risk-free rate of interest, R_F.

3. All investors have made identical subjective estimates of the means, variances, and covariances of returns among all available assets.

4. All assets are perfectly divisible and are marketable free of transactions costs.

5. There are no taxes.

6. All investors are price-takers in a perfectly competitive asset market.

7. The total quantity of all assets in the opportunity set is given and fixed, each such asset being uniquely defined, as implied by assumption 3, by a universally agreed subjectively assigned probability distribution of returns.

8. Each individual enters the market with a given wealth endowment, which he proceeds to distribute over the asset opportunity set in a manner that is optimal in the utility theoretic sense.

9. No changes occur in the asset opportunity set during the single market period, it being assumed that corporate firms neither issue new securities nor withdraw previously outstanding securities from the market. It is assumed that their investment and financing decisions have already been made.

Only brief comments need be made on the assumptions at this point. The first assumption invokes the preceding analysis of the risk-aversion utility function and its implications for optimum portfolio decisions. The second assumption is an analogue of the separation theorem, which depended on the assumption of an exogenously given market rate of interest.

The separation theorem depends also on the third assumption, that of "homogeneous expectations." This, it will emerge, is necessary in order to obtain from the theory a uniquely definable, "utility-free," optimum portfolio of risky assets whose return we denoted previously as R_M. Attempts have been made to dispense with the assumption of homogeneous expectations, for example by Lintner, but in such cases theoretical complications of a high order follow.[6] Lintner has shown that the introduction of heterogeneous expectations does not damage the qualitative form of the outcome, given the remaining assumptions of the model. But the full description of market equilibrium conditions then involves weighted averages of all investors' expectations. The Lintner argument reveals that the equilibrium condition involves

[6]John Lintner, "The Aggregation of Investors' Diverse Judgment and Preferences in Purely Competitive Securities Markets," *Journal of Financial and Quantitative Analysis* 4 (December 1969).

combinations of individual investors' marginal rates of substitution between risk and return, so that it is not then possible to eliminate utility information and obtain equilibrium relationships stated solely in terms of observable market parameters.[7] The market equilibrium prices and yields would not then be "utility-free," and the equilibrium theoretic model has continued to rely on the assumption of homogeneous expectations.

The assumption of perfect financial asset markets is expressed in both the perfect divisibility and marketability of assets, and in the unlimited borrowing and lending opportunities at a risk-free rate of interest. Reasons will emerge for suggesting that the perfect market assumption does not hold good in fact.

Difficulties arise also in connection with the assumed givenness of the asset opportunity set. In the movement and changes in the economic state of affairs firms also change. They expand, merge, decline, and die, and the volume and kinds of their capital securities outstanding also change, with traceable implications for financial investors' market opportunities.

Similar observations might be made regarding the assumptions of the givenness of investors' wealth endowments and the separateness of firms' investment and financing decisions from what transpires in the financial markets. These assumptions, taken together, imply also what Fama and Miller bring out most clearly and explicitly, namely the assumption that the market's movement toward its equilibrium posture takes place "through a process of tatonnement with recontracting."[8]

But at this stage we are interested in the logical validity of the conclusions that follow from the theory's own assumptions. The validity in that sense we do not call in question, and we can proceed therefore to the results that can be established on the basis of it.

Portfolio Asset Choice

Recall now the argument of the preceding chapter regarding the investor's problem of optimum portfolio selection. The efficient boundary of the investment opportunity set, *EE* in Figure 4 provided also the related concept of portfolio dominance. Specifying the risk inherent in an asset portfolio by the standard deviation of the return on the

[7]Cf. the discussion of the heterogeneous expectations assumption in Jensen, "Capital Markets," p. 390. We might point out in connection with the proposition in the text above that if all investors had utility functions of a form which exhibited "constant absolute risk-aversion" in the Pratt-Arrow sense, then it would be possible to obtain a solution condition expressed in terms of the given constant marginal rate of substitution and exogenous parameters. Cf. the discussion in Jensen.

[8]Fama and Miller, *Theory of Finance*, p. 278.

portfolio, and invoking previous notation with X_i, X_j representing the asset weights in the portfolio, the asset choice problem becomes that of finding solution values for the X_i in a minimum value of $\sigma(R_P) = (\Sigma_i\Sigma_j X_i \sigma_{ij})^{\frac{1}{2}}$, subject to a desired and specified rate of portfolio return.

This portfolio choice problem is that of minimizing $\sigma(R_P)$ subject to the constraint that $E(R_P) = \Sigma_i x_i E(R_i)$, and takes the following mathematical form.

$$\operatorname*{Min}_{x_i} \theta = \left[\sum_i^n \sum_j^n x_i x_j \sigma_{ij}\right]^{\frac{1}{2}} + \lambda_1 \left[E(R_P) - \sum_i^n x_i E(R_i)\right] + \lambda_2 \left[1 - \sum_i^n x_i\right]. \quad (6)$$

The second constraint takes account of the fact that the asset weights in the portfolio must sum to unity. (In Equation [6] and throughout the following analysis the tilde has been dropped from the random variables for notational economy.)

If a specified rate of return, $E(R_P)$, is introduced into the first constraint condition in the equation and the solution values of the x_i weights consistent with that rate of return are calculated, the resulting portfolio will be described by a point on the efficient portfolio locus, *EE*, of Figure 4. By varying the level of $E(R_P)$ to which this first constraint in Equation (6) is anchored the entire portfolio locus can be generated.[9] It is this boundary locus, or this market tradeoff between risk and return, that determines in part the market's optimum portfolio of risky assets and the equilibrium market price of risk.

An asset's *own* or *intrinsic* risk has been defined in terms of the variance of the subjectively assigned probability distribution of that asset's rate of return. But we must take account also of the covariances between that asset's return and the returns of all the other assets in the portfolio of which it is a member. The risk of an asset becomes measurable, then, by the contribution which a unit of that asset makes to the risk of the total portfolio in which it is included, or by $\partial\sigma(R_P)/\partial x_i$.

There will be occasion to use in what follows two other equivalent expressions for the same idea. Thus

$$\begin{aligned}\sigma(R_P) &= \left[\sum_i \sum_j x_i x_j \sigma_{ij}\right]^{\frac{1}{2}} \\ &= \sigma^2(R_P)/\sigma(R_P) \\ &= \frac{\Sigma_i \Sigma_j x_i x_j \sigma_{ij}}{\sigma(R_P)} \\ &= \Sigma x_i \frac{\Sigma x_j \sigma_{ij}}{\sigma(R_P)},\end{aligned}$$

[9]For the computational procedures and the techniques for computational economy, see William F. Sharpe, "A Simplified Model for Portfolio Analysis," *Management Science* (January 1963), and the same author's *Portfolio Theory and Capital Markets.*

from which it follows that

$$\frac{\partial\sigma(R_P)}{\partial x_i} = \frac{\Sigma x_j\sigma_{ij}}{\sigma(R_P)}. \tag{7}$$

From a different viewpoint the covariance between an asset's return and the return on the portfolio can be written as

$$\text{Cov}\,(R_i,\, R_P) = \text{Cov}\,(R_i,\, \Sigma x_j R_j) = \Sigma x_j\, \text{Cov}\,(R_i,\, R_j). \tag{8}$$

Substituting this equivalence into the numerator of Equation (7) provides the expression:

$$\frac{\partial\sigma(R_P)}{\partial x_i} = \frac{\text{Cov}\,(R_i,\, R_P)}{\sigma(R_P)}. \tag{9}$$

Our three formulations of the risk of an asset are then as follows:

$$\text{The risk of the } i\text{th asset} = \frac{\partial\sigma(R_P)}{\partial x_i} \tag{10}$$

$$= \frac{\Sigma x_j\sigma_{ij}}{\sigma(R_P)} \tag{11}$$

$$= \frac{\text{Cov}\,(R_i,\, R_P)}{\sigma(R_P)}. \tag{12}$$

The Risk-Free Asset Opportunity

Consider again the concave portfolio opportunity locus. If the investor was required to invest his entire wealth endowment in the opportunity set of risky assets, he would be confronted with the task of deciding which of all the efficient portfolios he should choose from the points on the efficient boundary. By marrying the investor's family of iso-utility indifference curves with the investment opportunity locus, a search could be made for the portfolio point at which tangency occurred. At that point the subjectively acceptable MRS between risk and return would be equal to the objectively attainable marginal rate of transformation between risk and return.

But in fact the investor is not in this way constrained to invest only in risky assets. It is assumed by the theory that he may place a part or the whole of his wealth endowment in a risk-free asset yielding a riskless rate of return R_F. As shown in Figure 10, let us imagine that an investor was to divide his investable endowment between the risk free asset yielding a return of R_F and portfolio A, which promises a return of $E(R_A)$, not shown in the figure, and presents a degree of risk $\sigma(R_A)$. The investor's return on his overall wealth portfolio position, assuming a proportion w was placed in the risk-free asset, would be

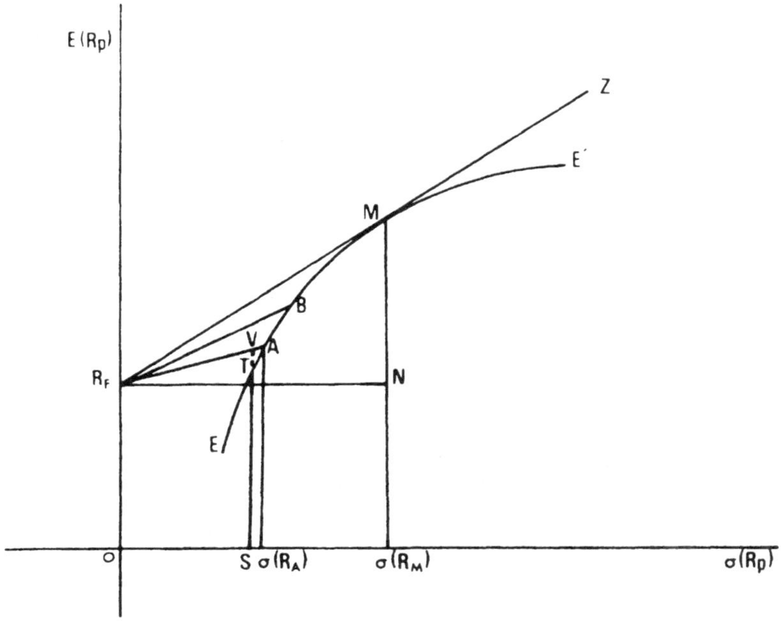

Figure 10.

$$E(R_P) = wR_F + (1 - w)\,E(R_A). \tag{13}$$

Similarly, his overall portfolio risk would be

$$\sigma^2(R_P) = (1 - w)^2\sigma^2(R_A)$$

or

$$\sigma(R_P) = (1 - w)\,\sigma(R_A). \tag{14}$$

Differentiating Equations (13) and (14) with respect to w and dividing the first such result by the second yields

$$\frac{dE(R_P)}{d\sigma(R_P)} = \frac{E(R_A) - R_F}{\sigma(R_A)}. \tag{15}$$

Given the probabilistic description of portfolio opportunity A, all terms on the right hand side of Equation (15) are known, and the *effective* portfolio opportunity locus described by the various possible proportionate combinations of R_F and A is described by the *linear* locus R_FA.

The existence of this opportunity implies that the *new* portfolio locus R_FA *dominates* that portion of the previously existing locus EE' which lies to the southwest of A. For in exchange for a risk exposure of

OS, for example, the EE' locus offers an expected return of ST, while the new linear locus offers a prospective return at that risk level of SV, indicating clearly a dominant portfolio.

The introduction of the risk-free asset opportunity has therefore transformed the efficient portfolio boundary from EE' to an *effective* efficient opportunity locus of R_FAE'. If, in the same way, the investor were to contemplate combinations of the risk-free asset and portfolio opportunity B, he could achieve a dominating locus of R_FB, and effective opportunity locus of R_FBE'. By experimenting in a similar fashion with other possible risky asset portfolios the investor could discover an *optimum portfolio of risky assets* with which the risk-free asset could be combined. Such a portfolio is designated as M in Figure 10, at which point the linearized locus is tangential to the previously existing EE' boundary. The investor's effective opportunities are then described by R_FME'.

To the extent that the investor is allocating his wealth between the risk-free asset and the optimum portfolio of risky assets M, he is *lending* at the risk-free rate of interest. Depending on his decision as to the proportion of his wealth which he should lend at this rate, he will settle at a point on the linear segment R_FM. But suppose also that the investor could *borrow* at the same risk-free rate. Then he could increase his expected return even further, at the same time undertaking additional risk, by borrowing at the risk-free rate and investing the proceeds in the risky portfolio M. In such an event he would settle somewhere on the MZ portion of what is now a completely linearized opportunity locus RMZ.[10] This locus may now be referred to as the Capital Market Line.

Given the assumption of homogeneous expectations, every investor who holds risky assets will choose to invest part of his wealth in portfolio M, and this is then what we have referred to as the market portfolio. This portfolio's expected return and risk were referred to in Equations (1) through (3) as $E(R_M)$ and $\sigma(R_M)$ respectively. The market portfolio M must be made up of *all* the assets in the risky opportunity set, and the proportion each asset occupies in the portfolio must equal the ratio of its market value to the total market value of all the assets combined. It is impossible for an asset, say the jth asset in the set, to account for a proportion of their total market value of all risky assets that is different from the proportion of their risky investments that all investors combined place in that asset. In full equilibrium, all the

[10]A logical difficulty enters at this point. If the individual borrows in the fashion suggested he will by doing so be issuing new securities, and will thus be increasing the total number of financial assets outstanding, in contradiction of the initial assumption that for purposes of the equilibrium model the supply of assets was given and fixed.

assets will be held by willing holders, the amounts borrowed will be offset by amounts lent, net borrowing will be zero, and all assets must be held by somebody.[11]

The Equilibrium Condition

Consider now the portfolio selection or the optimum asset choice problem summarized in Equation (6). Differentiating this objective function with respect to x_i and x_j and setting the partials equal to zero for first order extremum conditions yields

$$\frac{\partial \theta}{\partial x_i} = \frac{\partial \sigma(R_P)}{\partial x_j} - \lambda_1 E(R_i) - \lambda_2 = 0; \tag{16}$$

$$\frac{\partial \theta}{\partial x_j} = \frac{\partial \sigma(R_P)}{\partial x_j} - \lambda_1 E(R_j) - \lambda_2 = 0. \tag{17}$$

It follows from Equations (16) and (17) that

$$\frac{\partial \sigma(R_P)}{\partial x_i} - \lambda_1 E(R_i) = \frac{\partial \sigma(R_P)}{\partial x_j} - \lambda_1 E(R_j)$$

or that

$$E(R_j) - E(R_i) = \frac{1}{\lambda_1}\left[\frac{\partial \sigma(R_P)}{\partial x_j} - \frac{\partial \sigma(R_P)}{\partial x_i}\right]. \tag{18}$$

From the mathematical interpretation of Equation (6), λ_1 describes the partial derivative of the minimand function with respect to the constraint variable to which the λ_1 is attached, or $\lambda_1 = \partial\sigma(R_P)/\partial E(R_P)$. We can investigate now the nature of the portfolio extremum conditions at the optimum risky portfolio point M, and in the further development of the conditions in Equations (16) and (17) we can replace $E(R_P)$ and $\sigma(R_P)$ by $E(R_M)$ and $\sigma(R_M)$.

The solution value of λ_1 at the extremum in view can be linked to the fact that $\partial\sigma(R_M)/\partial E(R_M)$ is the reciprocal of the slope of the capital market line, $R_F M$, in Figure 10. This latter magnitude, $MN/R_F N$ in the Figure, is interpretable as $[E(R_M) - R_F]/\sigma(R_M)$. As an alternative formulation of the market price of risk it indicates the increment of return the market is providing in equilibrium for a unit change in portfolio risk.

Substituting this equivalent expression for λ_1 in Equation (18), multiplying the result by all x_i and adding the derived equations, we obtain the following aggregated expression:

[11]Cf. Sharpe, *Portfolio Theory and Capital Markets*, p. 82.

$$\Sigma x_i E(R_j) - \Sigma x_i E(R_i) = \frac{E(R_M) - R_F}{\sigma(R_M)} \left[\Sigma x_i \frac{\partial \sigma(R_M)}{\partial x_j} - \Sigma x_i \frac{\partial \sigma(R_M)}{\partial x_i} \right]. \quad (19)$$

Recalling that Σx_i equals unity in the first term on the left-hand side and also in the first term in the brackets on the right-hand side of Equation (19), it follows that

$$E(R_j) - E(R_M) = \frac{E(R_M) - R_F}{\sigma(R_M)} \left[\frac{\text{Cov}\,(R_j R_M)}{\sigma(R_M)} - \frac{\Sigma x_i \Sigma x_j \sigma_{ij}}{\sigma(R_M)} \right]. \quad (20)$$

In deriving this expression we have substituted Equations (12) and (11) into the first and second terms respectively in the brackets in Equation (19). The last term in Equation (20) can be recognized as the variance of return on the market portfolio divided by its own standard deviation, or simply as the standard deviation of the market portfolio return.

This last equivalence enables us to remove the bracket from Equation (20), with the following result:

$$E(R_j) - E(R_M) = R_F - E(R_M) + \left[\frac{E(R_M) - R_F}{\sigma(R_M)} \right] \cdot \frac{\text{Cov}\,(R_j, R_M)}{\sigma(R_M)}. \quad (21)$$

And Equation (21) may then be simplified to provide

$$E(R_j) = R_F + [E(R_M) - R_F] \cdot \frac{\text{Cov}\,(R_j, R_M)}{\sigma^2(R_M)}. \quad (22)$$

But the final covariance-variance ratio on the right-hand side of this equation is precisely what we referred to at the beginning of this chapter as β_j, the *j*th firm's beta coefficient, or the analogue of the empirical regression coefficient of the *j*th asset's rate of return on the rate of return on the market portfolio. Thus Equation (22) may be rewritten as

$$E(R_j) = R_F + \beta_j[E(R_M) - R_F], \quad (23)$$

which is the same as that originally presented in Equation (1) as the principal result of the equilibrium theory of financial asset prices. When full general equilibrium conditions in the financial asset market are satisfied, that is to say, the equilibrium yield on the *j*th risky asset is a linear function of the market risk premium.

The foregoing analysis is based on the assumption that all investors are mean-variance portfolio optimizers, making their asset choices against risk-aversion utility functions defined over the arguments of the mean and the variance of the possible portfolio outcomes. It was this utility theoretic assumption that enabled us to formulate the problem in the basic form of Equation (6).

The investor's mean-variance utility function may be written in the form $U = U[E(R_P), \sigma(R_P)]$. Its first order extremum condition with respect to the jth asset in the investor's portfolio, where x_j now represents the proportion of his *total wealth* placed in the jth risky asset, is

$$\frac{\partial U}{\partial E(R_P)} \cdot \frac{\partial E(R_P)}{\partial x_j} + \frac{\partial U}{\partial \sigma(R_P)} \cdot \frac{\partial \sigma(R_P)}{\partial x_j} = 0. \tag{24}$$

It follows that

$$\frac{\partial E(R_P)}{\partial x_j} = - \frac{\partial U/\partial \sigma(R_P)}{\partial U/\partial E(R_P)} \cdot \frac{\partial \sigma(R_P)}{\partial x_j}. \tag{25}$$

The first term on the right hand side of Equation (25) is recognizable as the investor's MRS between risk and return, which must be equal in equilibrium to the market price of risk or the slope of the capital market line. Using previous notation, at the point of utility optimization

$$\frac{\partial E(R_P)}{\partial x_j} = \frac{E(R_M) - R_F}{\sigma(R_M)} \cdot \frac{\partial \sigma(R_P)}{\partial x_j}. \tag{26}$$

We can visualize the investor's overall wealth allocation problem as being solved by placing a proportion of his wealth equal to Σx_j in a *risky* asset portfolio and the balance, $1 - \Sigma x_j$, in a risk-free asset yielding a return as before of R_F. The investor's expected return and risk exposure then become

$$E(R_P) = \Sigma x_j E(R_j) + (1 - \Sigma x_j)R_F \text{ and} \tag{27}$$

$$\sigma(R_P) = \left(\sum_i \sum_j x_i x_j \sigma_{ij}\right)^{\frac{1}{2}}. \tag{28}$$

Differentiation of Equations (27) and (28) provides:

$$\frac{\partial E(R_P)}{\partial x_j} = E(R_j) - R_F \text{ and} \tag{29}$$

$$\frac{\partial \sigma(R_P)}{\partial x_j} = \frac{\Sigma x_i \sigma_{ij}}{\sigma(R_M)}, \tag{30}$$

recalling, in the final term of Equation (30), that the portfolio on which interest can be focused when equilibrium conditions are satisfied is once again the market portfolio.

Equations (29) and (30) may then be substituted into the utility extremum condition in Equation (26) to provide:

$$E(R_j) - R_F = \frac{[E(R_M) - R_F]}{\sigma(R_M)} \cdot \frac{\Sigma x_i \sigma_{ij}}{\sigma(R_M)}. \tag{31}$$

In the final term of this equation the risk of the jth asset in the portfolio is recognizable from the result established in Equation (11). From Equation (31), using Equation (12),

$$E(R_j) - R_F = [E(R_M) - R_F] \cdot \frac{\text{Cov}(R_j, R_M)}{\sigma^2(R_M)}. \tag{32}$$

But this, of course, states again that when full general equilibrium conditions are satisfied the market's required risk premium on the jth risky asset will be a linear function of the risk premium on the market portfolio.

Our analysis has established that the determination of the market portfolio is "utility-free," and by this it is meant that given the risk-free rate of return R_F in Figure 10, portfolio M is determinable purely by portfolio mean-variance optimization conditions, quite independently of the magnitudes of utility any individual investor may attach to different possible outcomes, or the magnitudes that might similarly be attached to the marginal risk-return tradeoff at any point.

The uniqueness of the market portfolio M depends also on the assumption of homogeneous expectations, or the assumption that the investment opportunity set is itself uniquely defined in terms of the universally agreed probabilistic characteristics of the assets contained within it. This homogeneous expectations assumption should be seen as an *equilibrium* condition, and the adoption of it confirms the inapplicability of the model to the explanation of the *trading* that actually takes place in the real-world financial markets.

Wealth Allocation Separation Theorem

Let it be assumed now that all relevant conditions in the financial asset market are such that the optimum portfolio of risky assets has been determined at point M in Figure 11. It then follows that the investor's decision as to the division of his wealth endowment between this risky portfolio and the risk-free asset will be dependent on the form of his utility function, in particular on the degree of risk-aversion it exhibits. If, for example, the form of the indifference curves is such that the relevant point of tangency is established at M in Figure 11, the individual would place his entire wealth endowment in the risky portfolio.

If, on the other hand, the utility function exhibited a higher degree of risk aversion and established tangency at point S, the investor would divide his wealth between the risky portfolio and the risk-free asset. The rate of return on his total wealth position that he could expect as a result, and the overall risk to which he would be exposed,

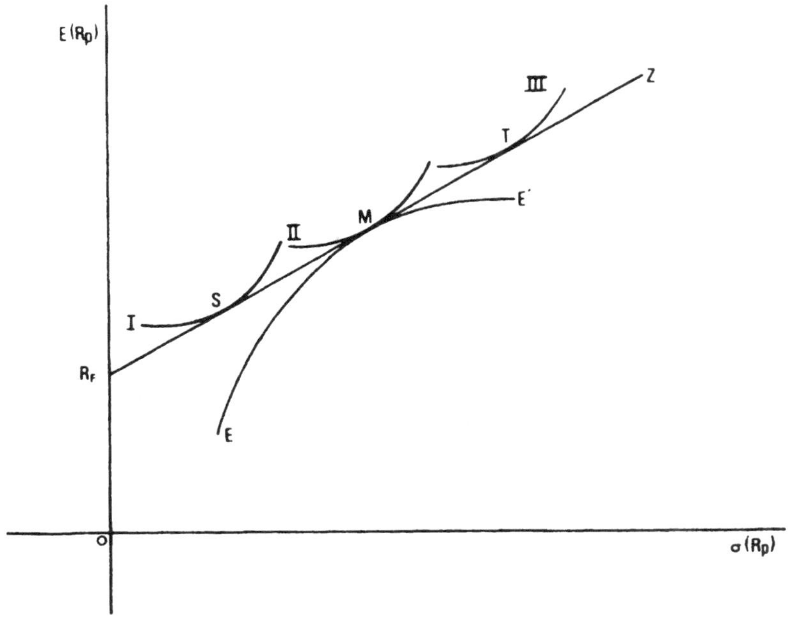

Figure 11.

would be described by the intercepts on the axes (not shown in the Figure) adjacent to S. If the investor, instead of investing in the risk-free asset and thereby *lending* at the given interest rate R_F, were to *borrow* at that rate and invest the proceeds in the risky portfolio, he might optimize at point *T* on the R_FMZ opportunity line. This could be the case if his utility function exhibited a somewhat lower degree of risk-aversion. The investor would then be increasing his expected return above that obtainable on the market portfolio *M*, but he would be increasing the degree of risk to which he was exposed. His expected return and risk are indicated by the intercepts on the coordinate axes adjacent to point *T*.

This, therefore, establishes the wealth allocation separation theorem. The investor's final decision regarding the distribution of his wealth endowment is *separable from* the decision as to the structure of the optimum portfolio of risky assets. The result is dependent on the assumption that all investors can borrow or lend any desired amount at an exogenously given risk-free rate of interest in perfect money capital markets. But a number of difficulties may arise in this connection.

It is quite conceivable that the assumption of market perfection does not provide a reasonable basis from which to begin an analysis of the possible outcomes of the trading that takes place in it. There may be quasi-monopsonistic and monopolistic phenomena on the respective sides of the market, and neither transactions nor the gathering of information may be costless. It may well be the case also that the risk-free rate of interest is unstable, for as we have seen, the speculative demand for liquidity and its intrinsic instabilities pervaded Keynes's analysis of the financial markets and the theory of the rate of interest.

The final results of the equilibrium theory of financial asset prices are therefore such that when the equilibrium conditions are satisfied three situations obtain. First, and assuming that we can rule out a corner solution in which the investor's entire wealth would be placed in the risk-free asset, all investors will hold the *same* portfolio of risky assets. Second, the proportionate distribution of their wealth will depend on the degree of risk-aversion in their assumed mean-variance utility function. Third, all investors will exhibit the *same* subjective marginal rates of substitution between risk and return, equal to the slope of the objectively determined linearized market opportunity locus.

Economic Time and Portfolio Horizons

Two issues warrant further comment before proceeding. The first has to do with a potentially serious methodological ambiguity in the theory as presented, and the second involves an aspect of what was referred to previously as economic time.

The theory, it must be emphasized, is completely static, presenting a static picture of a severely conceptualized state of a hypothetical world. As such, its epistemological potential is exhausted in the description of the relations that *would* exist *if* certain conditions consistent with the assumptions of the theory were *also* to be satisfied, and if all economic entities encompassed in the theory had been brought, by a process not at all specified in the theory, to a position of rest and mutually optimized satisfaction. The theory describes the postures that would exist *if* consistent *equilibrium conditions* in the financial asset market were to obtain, so that no further trading in financial assets need therefore occur.

But the results of the theory are presented in terms of functional relations between variables and a careful distinction therefore needs to be preserved between the *substance* of what is being stated and the *semantic form* in which the statement is made. For the result should in no sense be allowed to convey the impression that if a change should occur in *a* firm's or in *an* economic decision maker's position or descriptive data, then *that* economic entity could be expected to move along what appears to be the functional forms describing the results of the theory. It is beyond the competence of the theory entirely to say anything about *change* in this sense at all.

If *different* firms or *different* economic entities or decision makers were describable by *different* relevant data *at the same point in time,* then certain aspects of their *simultaneous* equilibrium posture could be deduced from the relations the theory establishes. But if *change* occurs, if data inputs to the relations undergo a *change over time,* then by the very meaning of the equilibrium theoretic methodology, variations must be envisaged in *all* of the mutually determined relations and outcomes in the scheme of things. And the theory itself is incompetent to say anything at all about what might transpire during the *process of change* and the new instabilities that might thereby be triggered.

The methodological ambiguity and the potential ambivalence in the interpretation of the results is no doubt compounded by the diagrammatic forms in which the analysis is expressed. The explanatory competence of the theory extends *not* to any statement about a *movement along* an apparently functional relation, but to the *hypothetical significance* of *simultaneously* observable *different* points *on* the function at a *given* point in time.

The question of economic time also comes again to the fore. The theory of asset portfolio selection as it has developed through the work of Markowitz, Tobin, Sharpe, Lintner, and others has bequeathed to the equilibrium financial market theory the assumptions that all investors are *single period* utility-of-wealth maximizers, that this single period is well defined, and that *all* investors envisage the *same* period of the *same* given time length. These assumptions necessarily follow from the *completely static* nature of the theory and from the fact that the theory has nothing to say about actual transactions taking place in actual time at all.

In the construction of the theory the *holding period* between the observation date and the time horizon to which the data are assumed to refer is *given.* In fact, however, the holding period over which asset portfolio positions are maintained is frequently the most important variable in the case, and it should hold a prominent place in the theoretical explanation of financial markets and their behavior. But in the canonical equilibrium theory the holding period is given and is not subject to variation at all. To this extent a principal subject of concern in actual market complexes has been avoided completely and assumed away by the theory.

The portfolio theory, as we have examined it, is based on the assumption that asset opportunities are exhaustively described in terms of subjectively assigned probability distributions of those assets' *periodic* rates of return. But it is well known that in actual fact the *realized holding period yield* obtained on an asset will depend on the actual length of calendar time over which it was held. In particular, capital gains realized from variations in holding periods may form a significant part of actual yields, and investor anticipations as to possible price movements (and therefore as to possible variations in holding periods) may constitute a meaningful motivation in the acquisition of assets or in the deletion of assets from existing portfolio positions. But the conventional portfolio theory, in its tidily probabilistic form, has abstracted from this important question entirely and has locked the analysis into assumedly given, uniform, constant, and universally agreed asset time horizons. Indeed, it is implicit in the argument that once a portfolio is determined as being mutually optimal for all investors it will be held forever.

If, on the contrary, an investor has the opportunity of realizing capital gains whenever he observes a price rise in the market for an asset, he may well be able to achieve a rate of return superior to that described by the mathematical expectation of the subjectively assigned probability distribution of single-period returns. And if account is taken of this fact or possibility, the portfolio theoretic foundation of the asset market theory collapses. In such a case it becomes difficult to sustain the proposition that the variance of the probability distribution of *periodic* returns as incorporated in the theory is a true or appropriate measure of risk.[12]

The damage done to the elegance and tidiness of asset market theory by the recognition of uncertainty and historic time is that from these sources speculation and the market impact of speculators enter the argument. The one thing that a speculator does not do in his entry to the financial asset market is to define *ab initio* a rigid holding period over which his asset position will be maintained. Just as the Tobin probabilistic-portfolio theoretic approach to liquidity demand was seen to be inadequate to accommodate the Keynesian theory, so the same portfolio theory remains suspect as a foundation for a theory of financial asset prices.[13]

[12]Victoria Chick has drawn my attention to an argument bearing on parts of the foregoing in Stephen Rousseas, *Monetary Theory* (New York: Knopf, 1972), pp. 267f.

[13]Tobin, "Liquidity Preference as Behavior Towards Risk."

6

Firm Financing and the Asset Market Model

This chapter will examine the stance of the corporate firm on the demand side of the money capital market, or as the supplier of the capital securities or financial assets whose equilibrium market prices and yields were examined in the preceding chapter.

Our understanding of the firm's financing and investment decision problems will be advanced by regarding it *not* as an entity within a generalized equilibrium economic structure, but as an entity whose decision problems evolve in *dis*equilibrium situations. It must decide at such points in time what is the constrained optimal or the best available next step that it might take.

If the nature of the capitalist process and the structure of industrial affairs were such that the firm could settle once and for all its product mix, its technological operating structure, its relative factor usage and real capital intensity, its market posture and its optimum financing mix, and if investment could thenceforth be "scale changing" investment only, then reliance could be placed for financing purposes on some such concept as a weighted average cost of money capital funds.[1] But the real problem arises because the matters we have just referred to describe precisely the things that *cannot* be supposed to be settled. Marshall's recognition that "the unexpected may happen," and Keynes's dictum with regard to many aspects of the future that "we simply do not know," alert us to see why criteria for action in the

[1]Cf. my discussion of the cost of money capital in Chapter 3, and note also the recent and extensive debates surrounding the weighted average cost of capital as referred to, for example, in the exchange of comments in the *Journal of Finance* 30 (June 1975). A further valuable summary appears in Timothy J. Nantell and C. Robert Carlson, "The Cost of Capital as a Weighted Average," *Journal of Finance* 30 (December 1975), and in Wilbur G. Lewellen, "A Conceptual Reappraisal of Cost of Capital," *Financial Management* 3 (Winter 1974).

business world must be based on the way things appear to decision makers in the actual conditions and at the time at which commitments have to be made.[2]

The context of the firm's financing decision in its uniquely describable milieu has led us to emphasize the *marginal* cost of relaxing the firm's money capital availability constraint, rather than to espouse an *average* capital cost criterion. If the step-by-step dynamics of the decision responsibility has any cogency at all, we must be interested consistently in the decision as to the most advisable *next* step to be made. This suggests *marginal* evaluation and a *marginal* criterion for action, for the decision situation is past forever when it is gone, and it is in the nature of economic time that that situation can not be recalled. The decision responsibility, therefore, is that of taking the optimal action at the existing margin of choice. As Shackle puts it, our "endless journey into the void of time" means that we shall never stand at precisely that decision point again.[3]

Something of the spirit of this viewpoint is evinced by Lewellen when he concludes that certain measures of the "weighted average cost of capital . . . may be appealing because they are convenient . . . but they serve no detectable analytic purpose."[4] Lewellen observes that "in fact, all precepts of incremental analysis specify that commitments previously made *and circumstances previously existing* have no necessary bearing on the wisdom of today's decisions."[5]

A failure to appreciate the significance of the firm's financing decision margin, and the apparent wish to shelter in the epistemological security of workable rules of thumb, have led to a deep mystique and an almost impenetrable argument on the meaning of the firm's cost of capital. This was defined in Chapter 3 as the minimum required rate of return that must be earned on an investment of marginal money capital in the firm in order to make the employment of it economically worthwhile, or in order, that is, to prevent any dilution of the economic wealth position of the owners.

From this it follows that the notion of "the cost of capital of firm X" (of, say, a firm listed on the New York Stock Exchange) has, in the abstract, no meaning at all. "The cost of capital" has no meaning, notwithstanding all the attempts in the literature to insist to the con-

[2]Marshall, *Principles of Economics*, p. 347; Keynes, "General Theory of Employment," p. 214.

[3]Shackle, *Years of High Theory* p. 149.

[4]Lewellen, "Conceptual Reappraisal," p. 67.

[5]Ibid., p. 65, my italics. For a further discussion of the "cutoff rate" for investment decision as "the *marginal* and not the *average* cost of capital" see Fred D. Anditti and Milford S. Tysseland, "Three Ways to Present the Marginal Cost of Capital," *Financial Management* 2 (1973).

trary, except as the financing cost in the manner we have just defined, in a *given* and *specific* decision situation, in a *definable* environment and milieu, and at a *specific* point in time. The purposes for which capital will be used will influence the degree of risk to which the suppliers of it will be exposed, the structure of the firm in which it is being put to work, and therefore the rates of return required by the lenders or investors.

It would therefore be superfluous at this time to enter the extensive debate on the specification of the firm's weighted average cost of capital. We have in any event shown that this concept itself can be meaningfully interpreted *only in an equilibrium situation,* or only when the firm is in an *optimum optimorum* structural situation.[6] But what *is* necessary at this time is to examine the manner in which the average capital cost concept is afforded a recurring recrudescence by applying certain results of the equilibrium theory of financial asset prices. We shall look briefly in this chapter at a small number of capital cost concepts and at the importation to the investment decision making criteria of the firm of the results of the asset pricing model.

Some Cost of Capital Concepts

Consider the following notation in connection with a firm's financing costs and financial structure: V, π, and ρ refer to the market value, profits, and capitalization rate applicable to the owners' equity or the shares of the firm's common stock capital. D, F, and r refer to the market value, interest earnings, and the average rate of interest on the debt capital of the firm. W and O refer to the total capitalized value, W, of the net operating income of the firm, O, and the relationship O/W will provide a measure of i, the notional or effective rate of capitalization at which the total earnings of the firm are being valued in W.

The following relations are implied in the foregoing definitions:

$$V = \pi/\rho,\ \pi = \rho V; \tag{1}$$

$$D = F/r,\ F = rD; \tag{2}$$

$$W = O/i,\ O = iW. \tag{3}$$

If, at any point in time, a set of security values and income statement items are observed, the following summary or definitional statements may be made:

[6]Cf. Vickers, "Cost of Capital and the Structure of the Firm," and my references in this connection in Chapter 3 above to Arzac, "Structural Planning under Controllable Business Risk."

$$i = \frac{O}{W} = \frac{F + \pi}{W}. \tag{4}$$

It follows by substitution of (1) and (2) that

$$i = r\frac{D}{W} + \rho\frac{V}{W}. \tag{5}$$

Recognizing that W is also the total market value of the firm's outstanding capital securities, Equation (5) may be written in a form that specifies the weighted average cost of capital. This then provides an interpretation of the notional capitalization rate, i:

$$i = r\left[\frac{D}{D + V}\right] + \rho\left[\frac{V}{D + V}\right]. \tag{6}$$

As a notional capitalization rate, i is not an observable variable in the financial asset or money capital market. The data which *are* observable are the r and the ρ capitalization rates, depending on market asset values and implicit required rates of return in the debt and equity sectors of the money capital market. It is conceivable, moreover, that an empirical and more or less stable relationship exists between these money capital costs. Consider the equity capitalization rate, ρ, in the foregoing definitions:

$$\rho = \frac{\pi}{V} = \frac{O - F}{V} = \frac{i(D + V)}{V} - \frac{rD}{V}.$$

From this it follows that

$$\rho = i + (i - r)D/V \tag{7}$$

This appears to present us with the proposition that the equity capitalization rate is a linear function of the debt-to-equity financing ratio, D/V, in the firm. In fact, Equations (6) and (7) contain the two principal propositions in corporate capital financing theory which were presented in the celebrated Modigliani and Miller paper and which have been the source of a very large debate.[7]

But care must be taken in the interpretation of the average capital cost and the equity capitalization rate formulas as derived in these

[7]Modigliani and Miller, "Cost of Capital." See also, for critical evaluations and the extensive debates in this area, Ezra Solomon, ed., *The Management of Corporate Capital* (Chicago: Free Press of Glencoe for the Graduate School of Business, Univ. of Chicago, 1959), and the same author's *The Theory of Financial Management* (New York: Columbia Univ. Press, 1963), Stephen H. Archer and Charles A. D'Ambrosio, eds., *The Theory of Business Finance: A Book of Readings* (New York: Macmillan, 1967), and the bibliography provided in the more recent Haley and Schall, *Theory of Financial Decisions.*

equations. These expressions should be rigorously understood as *definitional statements* implicit in the structure of things observable *at a given moment in time.* They do not in any sense provide a theory of the average cost of capital or a theory of the equity owners' required rate of return. In saying this, of course, we are making the same kind of statement as followed previously from our presentation of the equilibrium asset market conditions. Equations (6) and (7) present us with a set of *definitional relations* that necessarily exist between observable magnitudes relating to the firm's financing structure and operating performance at a point in time. It is beyond the competence of the statements we have so far made to convey any conclusion at all as to what would be the *change* in, say, the equity capital cost if a change were to occur in the underlying state of affairs.

We must avoid any statement about the manner in which a firm may be able to *move along* the apparent functional relation described in Equation (7). As will be seen more fully in what follows, the equation serves only to identify the relation which would exist *if conditions of equilibrium in the financial asset market were also assumed to exist.* We are not yet in possession of a *theory* of what might happen during a *process* of trading in the financial asset market when conditions of equilibrium do *not* exist. To move from the definitional propositions to a theory of financial capital costs it is necessary to introduce a set of behavior postulates purporting to describe the ways in which participants in the financial markets actually behave in conditions of change.

If we can assume that *perfect markets* exist, that no transactions costs or taxes are incurred, and that both firms and individuals can borrow at an externally given market rate of interest, then the following argument regarding a *possible* market equilibrating activity can be posited.[8]

Let it be supposed that two firms, A and B, of the same size, operating in the same industry in the same economic environment, both earn the same rate of return on the total capital invested, and that they both exhibit the same degree of risk in their respective income streams. The firms are assumed to be members of the same "risk class" as that concept has become familiar in the literature, and they differ only in the financing mix they have adopted.

[8]The assumptions invoked in this sentence should be carefully noted, and the violation of any one or more of them will be sufficient to invalidate the equilibrium conclusions, essentially the Modigliani-Miller conclusions, which we shall reach in what follows. For a discussion of transactions costs and market imperfections, see William J. Baumol and Burton G. Malkiel, "The Firm's Optimal Debt-Equity Combination and the Cost of Capital," *Quarterly Journal of Economics* 81 (November 1967).

We shall suppose that firm *A* has financed its asset investments completely from equity capital sources and that firm *B* has financed 50 percent of its requirements by means of debt capital. We shall assume that for both firms the internal rate of return on capital employed, or the ratio of the net operating income to the book value of total assets, is 10 percent. Finally, both the firm and its security holders can borrow at 4 percent, the total value of assets is $10,000, and no account is taken for the present of either corporate or personal taxes.

Our objective is to demonstrate that on the assumption of a smoothly functioning investor arbitrage mechanism in an assumedly perfect capital asset market, the total market value of the securities of the levered firm *B* cannot diverge permanently from the total market value of the unlevered firm *A*. If it is possible to sustain the proposition that the total market values of the respective firms' securities, *W*, must be equal, then for a given total income stream, $\bar{O}$, the ratio of $\bar{O}/W$ must be the same for both firms. The weighted average cost of capital for both firms, or $i = \bar{O}/W$, will then also be equal. It could be said in that case that the average cost of capital to the firm is invariant with respect to its financing mix. If, moreover, the average cost of capital is constant, the magnitude involved also specifies the *marginal* cost of capital, and the appropriate required rate of return for use as a capital expenditure decision criterion is also thereby specified.

Suppose, *ab initio*, that a "temporarily anomalous" situation exists in the financial asset market and that the securities of firm B are overvalued relative to those of firm A. We shall then exhibit the supposed arbitrage mechanism which corrects the anomaly and restores the equality of market values. Let the following situation obtain.

Table 1 indicates the sense in which firm B is assumed to be overvalued. Let us imagine now that an owner of 10 percent of the common stock of the levered firm B can sell his shares and purchase a 10

Table 1

	Firm A	*Firm B*
Total assets	$10,000	$10,000
Internal Rate of Return	10%	10%
Net operating Income	$1,000	$1,000
Market value of equity	$10,000	$6,000
Market value of debt	—	$5,000
Total market value of the firm's securities	$10,000	$11,000

percent ownership of the unlevered firm A, that is he can "arbitrage" in the firms' common stock securities. Given that such an investor will obtain $600 from the sale of his 10 percent ownership in firm B, and that he requires $1000 to acquire the contemplated 10 percent ownership of firm A, he will need to borrow the difference of $400 on his personal account, conceivably against the collateral of the equity stock of firm A, which he is about to acquire. Such borrowing, it has already been assumed, can be made at the same rate of interest as that at which debt capital funds are available to the firms. Consider, then, the income accruing to the investor from his alternative positions.

Table 2
Investor alternative income positions

	Income from a 10 percent ownership	
	Firm A	*Firm B*
Firm net operating income	$1,000	$1,000
Less debt interest at 4%	—	200
Residual equity income	1,000	800
10% equity income	100	80
Less interest on personal debt	16	—
Net portfolio income	84	80

Table 2 indicates that by selling his 10 percent ownership of the levered firm B and purchasing a corresponding proportionate ownership of the unlevered firm A the investor can increase his income prospects from $80 to $84. But as the market arbitrage proceeds, the selling pressure can be expected to reduce the market value of the firm B security, and the corresponding buying pressure will increase the value of Firm A. The motivation for arbitrage will disappear when the divergence of market values between firm A and firm B has been eliminated, and a common market value will then have established an equality of average capital costs. The income stream $\bar{O}$ being given for the two firms and the Ws having been brought into equality, the $i = \bar{O}/W$ must be the same for each of the firms.

A good many reasons can be adduced why things may not work out as smoothly as we have just supposed. Doubts may be expressed as to the ability of individuals and firms to borrow on comparable terms, or as to whether the investor, by thus substituting "home-made leverage" in his personal portfolio for what was previously a levered position by reason of the financial leverage in firm B's capital structure, has in fact maintained a strictly comparable risk exposure. The assumption of zero transactions costs and the assumed absence of corporate and capital gains taxes could also be questioned. But leaving aside these details, two aspects of the parable will be seen to give it a kinship with the static equilibrium asset pricing theory: the assumption of an exogenously given and fixed market rate of interest, and that of perfect financial market conditions. Additionally, if all firms in a given "risk class" exhibited the same average cost of capital, i, this would provide an empirical vindication of the analytical proposition that the financing cost is invariant with respect to the financing mix, and a basis would thereby be provided for a reliance on the posited linear form of the equity cost function described in Equation (7).

The methodological difference between the foregoing and our own way of looking at things can be put as follows. Instead of claiming that the cost of equity capital is what it is because the weighted average cost of capital is constant, we prefer to say that the empirically observable equity and debt costs provide the basis *from* which we argue, and the average cost function, so far as we are interested in it, is the conclusion *to* which we argue. Thus the cost of a firm's debt capital will be whatever it is observed to be by virtue of the supply and demand conditions in the debt capital sector of the money capital market, taking account of the degree of risk-aversion in the attitudes of the suppliers of debt capital funds. Similarly, the cost of equity capital will reflect conditions in the equity capital sector of the money capital market. Given, then, the separately observable debt and equity capital costs, their mutual relevance can be brought into focus in what we discussed in Chapter 3 as the full marginal cost of relaxing the firm's money capital availability constraint.

In our earlier analysis account was taken of the impact on the firm's marginal financing decision of the corporate income tax, which reduced the effective required rate of return on marginal money capital investment in the firm. If the corporate tax is taken into account in the present context, an adjustment of the capital cost relationships again occurs.

Using established notation, the tax deductibility of interest on debt capital implies that

$$\pi = (O - F)(1 - t) \tag{8}$$

and the total earnings after tax generated for the security holders becomes

$$\begin{aligned} \pi + F &= (O - F)(1 - t) + F \\ &= O(1 - t) + tF. \end{aligned} \tag{9}$$

Substituting $F = rD$ from Equation (2), and defining W_L as the total market value of the securities of the levered firm and $L = D/W_L$ as the degree of financial leverage in the firm's capital structure, it follows by capitalizing the total net earnings stream in Equation (9) that

$$W_L = \frac{O(1 - t)}{\rho} + tW_L L. \tag{10}$$

In this expression ρ is the equity capitalization rate that would be applied to the earnings stream of an all-equity firm, and the debt owners' component of the income stream has been capitalized at the debt cost rate of interest, r.

Equation (10) then provides an expression for the average cost of capital of the levered firm, ρ^*:

$$\rho(1 - tL) = \frac{O(1 - t)}{W_L} = \rho^*. \tag{11}$$

The corporate income tax thus effectively reduces the cost of capital to the firm.[9] By virtue of the tax deductibility of interest payments on the firm's debt capital, the total market value of a levered firm will, on the given assumptions of an arbitrage activity in perfect financial markets, exceed the market value of a comparable unlevered firm by $tW_L L$, representing the present capitalized value of the annual corporate tax saving.

Implications of the Asset Market Model

The assumptions of perfect financial markets and of an externally given rate of interest give the foregoing analysis a kinship with that of the equilibrium asset market model. The fact that the principal result of the asset pricing model can be transformed into the equity cost function in Equation (7) confirms that this last mentioned and widely espoused criterion is suspect on the very same grounds as the equilibrium theory.[10]

In the following development we assume again that firm A is completely equity financed with a market value V_A, and the expected rate of return on its equity ownership is

$$E(R_A) = E(X_A)/V_A \tag{12}$$

[9]For a view contrary to the essential Modigliani-Miller conclusion presented in the foregoing, cf. Bierman and Hass, *Introduction to Managerial Finance*, p. 170, n. 7.

[10]For a fuller discussion, cf. Robert S. Hamada, "Portfolio Analysis, Market Equilibrium and Corporation Finance," *Journal of Finance* 24 (March 1969), and Haley and Schall, *Theory of Financial Decisions* chapters 7 and 8. The following argument is indebted to these sources.

In this expression X_A refers to the annual stream of benefits resulting from holding the shares of common stock, including both dividends and capital gains (or losses).

In the case of the levered firm B, otherwise comparable with A, its borrowing will be assumed to take place at a given rate of interest R_F. Referring to its debt capital outstanding as D_B, ignoring corporate income taxes, and omitting the tildes from the random variables, the expected equity rate of return is

$$E(R_B) = \frac{E(X_A) - R_F D_B}{V_B}. \tag{13}$$

Now we recall that the principal result of the equilibrum theory of financial asset prices was previously stated as

$$E(R_j) = R_F + \lambda \operatorname{Cov}(R_j, R_M), \tag{14}$$

where λ was interpreted as the market price of risk, $[E(R_M) - R_F]/\sigma^2(R_M)$. Expressing Equations (12) and (13) in corresponding notation and making use of Equation (14) yields

$$\frac{E(X_A)}{V_A} = R_F + \lambda \operatorname{Cov}(R_A, R_M) \tag{15}$$

and

$$\frac{E(X_A) - R_F D_B}{V_B} = R_F + \lambda \operatorname{Cov}(R_B, R_M). \tag{16}$$

In these relationships, moreover,

$$\begin{aligned} \operatorname{Cov}(R_A, R_M) &= \operatorname{Cov}\left[\frac{X_A}{V_A}, R_M\right] \\ &= \frac{1}{V_A} \operatorname{Cov}(X_A, R_M) \end{aligned} \tag{17}$$

and

$$\begin{aligned} \operatorname{Cov}(R_B, R_M) &= \operatorname{Cov}\left[\frac{X_A - R_F \cdot D_B}{V_B}, R_M\right] \\ &= \frac{1}{V_B} \operatorname{Cov}(X_A, R_M). \end{aligned} \tag{18}$$

Substituting these equivalences into Equations (15) and (16) provides

$$E(R_A) = R_F + \frac{\lambda}{V_A} \operatorname{Cov}(X_A, R_M) \tag{19}$$

and

$$E(R_B) = R_F + \frac{\lambda}{V_B} \operatorname{Cov}(X_A, R_M). \tag{20}$$

Subtracting $E(R_A)$ from $E(R_B)$, understanding that the rate of return on the levered equity shares of firm B can be expected to exceed the rate of return available on the unlevered equity shares of firm A,

$$E(R_B) - E(R_A) = \lambda \operatorname{Cov}(X_A, R_M) \frac{(V_A - V_B)}{V_A V_B}. \tag{21}$$

If, now, Equations (15) and (16) are solved for $E(X_A)$ and the results equated, it follows that

$$V_A\left[R_F + \lambda \operatorname{Cov}(R_A, R_M)\right] = V_B\left[\lambda \operatorname{Cov}(R_B, R_M) + R_F \frac{(V_B + D_B)}{V_B}\right]. \tag{22}$$

In this expression we can substitute the equivalences in Equations (17) and (18) to provide:

$$V_A\left[R_F + \frac{\lambda}{V_A} \operatorname{Cov}(X_A, R_M)\right] =$$

$$V_B\left[\frac{\lambda}{V_B} \operatorname{Cov}(X_A, R_M) + R_F \frac{(V_B + D_B)}{V_B}\right]. \tag{23}$$

From Equation (23), then, it follows that

$$V_A R_F = V_B R_F + D_B R_F, \tag{24}$$

which implies that

$$V_A = V_B + D_B. \tag{25}$$

Equation (25) states that the asset pricing model from which it has been derived implies that *when the full equilibrium conditions are satisfied* the total market value of the levered firm B, shown as the sum of its equity and debt capital on the right-hand side of Equation (25) will be equal to the market value of a comparable unlevered firm as shown on the left-hand side of the equation. This is the same result as was established previously under the assumptions of a smoothly functioning arbitrage in a perfect financial market. The total market values of comparable levered and unlevered firms must be equal and invariant with respect to their financing mix.

Making use of this result, Equation (21) implies that

$$E(R_B) - E(R_A) = \lambda \operatorname{Cov}(X_A, R_M) \frac{D_B}{V_A V_B} \tag{26}$$

Inspection of Equation (19) indicates that *in the generalized equilibrium which the asset market model has in view,*

$$\lambda \operatorname{Cov}(X_A, R_M) = [E(R_A) - R_F]V_A \tag{27}$$

and Equation (27) may therefore be substituted into Equation (26) to yield:

$$E(R_B) - E(R_A) = [E(R_A) - R_F]\frac{D_B}{V_B}. \tag{28}$$

Rearranged, Equation (28) provides:

$$E(R_B) = E(R_A) + [E(R_A) - R_F]\frac{D_B}{V_B}. \tag{29}$$

Comparing this with Equation (7) confirms that the result thus derived from the equilibrium conditions of the asset pricing model, as in Equation (29), is the same as was vindicated in Equation (7) by arguing from the constancy of the weighted average cost of capital as supported by a posited arbitrage mechanism in a perfect financial asset market.

Investment Demand for Money Capital

The moral of the argument is that the extensive discussion in the theoretical literature of the average cost of capital and the recommendation of related variables as investment decision criteria in real-world firms are deeply embedded in the assumptions of the equilibrium model of financial asset markets. If the static assumptions of such a model are called in question, or if there is reason to believe that the decisions of the firm are made in *dis*equilibrium situations, then the entire structure of the cost of capital arguments collapses.[11]

To consider the implications of the theory for the investment expenditure criterion, recall the principal result in the following form:

$$E(\tilde{R}_j) = R_F + \lambda \operatorname{Cov}(\tilde{R}_j, \tilde{R}_M) \tag{30}$$

We indicate by X_{jt} in what follows the stream of benefits received during period t by the holder of a share of common stock of the jth firm, including dividend payments and realizable capital gains. Consistent with theoretical traditions in this area, we shall consider a single period model. In that case the rate of return on this jth asset is

$$\tilde{R}_j = \frac{\tilde{X}_j}{V_j} - 1 \tag{31}$$

where V_j describes the present value of the asset.

Taking the expected value of this rate of return we can observe that

[11]Parts of the following discussion of the investment and financing criteria implied by the equilibrium theory are dependent on Haley and Schall, *Theory of Financial Decisions*, q.v.

when full market equilibrium conditions are satisfied this expected return must also be describable by Equation (30), and by substitution a basic asset valuation relationship is obtained:

$$\frac{\bar{X}_j}{V_j} - 1 = R_F + \lambda \operatorname{Cov}\left[\left[\frac{\tilde{X}_j}{V_j} - 1\right], \tilde{R}_M\right] \tag{32}$$

From this it follows that

$$\bar{X}_j - V_j = V_j R_F + \lambda \operatorname{Cov}(\tilde{X}_j, \tilde{R}_M),$$

which can be reduced to

$$V_j = \frac{\bar{X}_j - \lambda \operatorname{Cov}(\tilde{X}_j, \tilde{R}_M)}{1 + R_F} \tag{33}$$

According to Equation (33), in *generalized market equilibrium* the value of an asset will be equal to (1) the present value of the future expected cash flow generated by the asset when that is discounted at a risk-free rate of interest, less (2) a discount for risk. The discount for risk is the similarly discounted value of the product of (a) the covariance between the cash flow generated by the asset and the rate of return on the market portfolio and (b) the market price of risk.

Now the cash flow generated by the firm in any period will be distributed, as discussed in Chapter 4, according to

$$\tilde{S}_t = \tilde{X}_t - F_t - I_t + \Delta D_t \tag{34}$$

where S, F, and I refer respectively to common stock dividends, debt service charges, and investment expenditures. If the investment decision is given, the size of the dividend payment will depend on any new debt issues ΔD_t, undertaken in partial financing of the investment expenditures.

Suppose that a firm which initially has no debt outstanding raises ΔD_0 at the current decision date, with an obligation to repay this amount with interest at a rate of r at the end of the single period operating horizon. The dividend stream can then be described as

$$S_0 = X_0 + \Delta D_0 - I_0 \tag{35}$$

and

$$\tilde{S}_1 = \tilde{X}_1 - \tilde{Y}_1, \tag{36}$$

where $Y_1 = (1 + r)\Delta D_0$ and is interpretable as a random variable because the underlying cash flow may be inadequate to service the debt obligation in full.

The basic valuation formula in Equation (33) enables us to write the present value of S_1 as

$$S_1 = \frac{(\bar{X}_1 - \bar{Y}_1) - \lambda \text{ Cov } [(\tilde{X}_1 - \tilde{Y}_1), \tilde{R}_M]}{1 + R_F}$$

$$= \frac{\bar{X}_1 - \lambda \text{ Cov } (\tilde{X}_1, \tilde{R}_M)}{1 + R_F} - \frac{\bar{Y}_1 - \lambda \text{ Cov } (\tilde{Y}_1, \tilde{R}_M)}{1 + R_F}. \quad (37)$$

From the basic valuation formula the final term on the righthand side of Equation (37) will equal ΔD_0, for under equilibrium conditions the suppliers of the incremental debt capital will be prepared to pay for the securities, in the assumedly perfect asset market, the present valuation of their expected stream of cash flow benefits.

Rewriting this last term in Equation (37) and adding it to the Equation (35), the wealth which the firm provides to its owners from its operations is

$$W_0 = S_0 + S_1 = X_0 + \Delta D_0 - I_0 + \frac{\bar{X}_1 - \lambda \text{ Cov } (\tilde{X}_1, \tilde{R}_M)}{1 + R_F} - \Delta D_0 \quad (38)$$

This reduces to

$$W_0 = X_0 - I_0 + \frac{\bar{X}_1 - \lambda \text{ Cov } (\tilde{X}_1, \tilde{R}_M)}{1 + R_F} \quad (39)$$

Equation (39) confirms that the stockholders' wealth position is dependent only on the underlying cash flow generating ability of the firm and its given investment policy, reflecting in a new guise the basic separation theorem of Chapter 4. As the debt financing term does not appear in Equation (39), the same kind of separation theorem argument again conveys the doctrine that with a given investment policy the financing mix adopted by the firm is irrelevant to the stockholders' interests.

To establish the firm's incremental capital investment expenditure criterion we can now use Equation (39). X'_1 now designates the cash flow which would be generated by the firm if no incremental investment were undertaken at the current decision moment, that is, if I_0 equals zero, and ΔX is the incremental cash flow which would result from a positive current investment. The stockholders' wealth position is then defined as

$$W_0 = X_0 - I_0 + \frac{(\bar{X}'_1 + \Delta\bar{X}) - \lambda \text{ Cov } [(\tilde{X}'_1 + \Delta\tilde{X}), \tilde{R}_M]}{1 + R_F} \quad (40)$$

or

$$W_0 = X_0 + \frac{\bar{X}'_1 - \lambda \text{ Cov } (\tilde{X}'_1, \tilde{R}_M)}{1 + R_F} + \frac{\Delta\bar{X} - \lambda \text{ Cov } (\Delta\tilde{X}, \tilde{R}_M)}{1 + R_F} - I_0. \quad (41)$$

The last two terms on the right-hand side of Equation (41) provide the incremental investment project decision criterion. For a proposed investment expenditure I_M with an expected marginal cash inflow of M, the decision criterion is

$$\frac{\bar{M} - \lambda \text{ Cov } (\bar{M}, \tilde{R}_M)}{1 + R_F} \geq I_M. \tag{42}$$

The potentially very general nature of this criterion should be noted. It does not say that the incremental investment must necessarily be "scale-changing" investment only. The criterion focuses on marginal investment outlays, and ***provided the new project is economically independent of the firm's existing activities,*** it is claimed that it may be evaluated in accordance with the criterion of Inequality (42). By *economic independence* it is meant that the adoption of the project does not affect the probability of any outcome from any other project of the firm. Provided this condition of economic independence is satisfied, the project may then be valued at the same value as would be placed upon it if it were sold as a separate entity in the financial asset market.

Economic independence does not necessarily imply, nor need we be concerned with, *statistical* independence. The firm's decision makers do not have to be concerned at all with statistical dependence between its project activities, provided only that they are economically independent. The firm, in other words, does *not* have a portfolio problem. Only its shareholders have a portfolio problem.

Given, in accordance with the assumptions of the asset market model, that the shareholders can engage in portfolio diversification, the covariance relationship in the basic valuation formula and in the investment criterion takes full account, ***in a situation of generalized market equilibrium,*** of the impact of the firm's decisions on the risk exposure of its owners. The latter, given only the opportunities for optimum risky portfolio construction, may achieve any desired level of risk exposure they wish.

It is not necessary for our purposes to take the parable further. But a conclusion similar to the foregoing holds in regard to the advisability or otherwise of mergers between firms. It might be thought, *prima facie,* that the justification for diversified merger activity lay in the advantages that might accrue from distributing investable resources over income earning opportunities whose prospective income streams were less than perfectly, and conceivably negatively, correlated. But the propositions we have adduced in this section imply, on the contrary, that provided the elements of the merger arrangement are economically independent, or provided, to use familiar terminology, that no economic "synergism" results from the merger, then the diversification problem can be left to the firm's shareholders to solve for themselves in the now familiar portfolio theoretic manner. The firm need have no regard to the question in its own structural decisions at all. In considering a firm's investment decision, Bierman and Hass noted that "the relevant risk consideration" is "the relation of the risk of the investment to the market risk. *The firm's risk position is not relevant.*"[12] Such results, however, are based on all the assumptions and conditions of the equilibrium asset market theory.

A Partial Critique

Bearing in mind its parentage in the equilibrium theory and the derivation of the investment criterion in Inequality (42), the cogency and viability of the criterion can be questioned on a number of grounds. We may consider its logical coherence, its empirical relevance or applicability, and the respect in which reliance upon it may in fact point to the elimination of the very meaning and significance of business management responsibility.

On the matter of logic, consider the risk discount component of the formulation. The λ in the expression is purportedly describing the *equilibrium market price of risk.* This, then, is in strict logic dependent on the satisfaction of all of the assumptions and conditions of the equilibrium model. The equilibrium market price of risk is perforce generated by a "pure exchange" mechanism operating within a *given and defined asset investment opportunity set.* But we can recall the methodological warning that the explanatory competence of the model does not extend beyond the specification of equilibrium *conditions,* and no statements can be made on the basis of it regarding a *process* of change when the underlying conditions are disturbed.

On the first point, however, the new investment made by a firm means that the financial investors' asset opportunity set is *not* any longer fixed and well defined, and therefore the logical relevance of a market price of risk based on the assumption of a given opportunity set evaporates. Corporate investment and new financing may add new securities to the existing asset set; and the new investment may change the subjectively assigned probabilistic characteristics in terms of which the existing opportunity set is defined.

The market price of risk, in short, is not independent of the new investment and financing in relation to which it is proposed to import it as a criterion. This problem, of course, may be avoided by assumption. The new investment may be so small in relation to the existing market opportunities that its effect on the price of risk may be ignored. That may or may not be reasonable. But it is in any event a matter of

[12]Harold Bierman, Jr., and Jerome E. Hass, "Capital Budgeting under Uncertainty: A Reformulation," *Journal of Finance* 28 (March 1973), p. 127, our italics; cf. the same authors' *Introduction to Managerial Finance*, p. 230.

empirical supposition and not of logic. As changes occur over time the cumulative effects may become significant, and on any given day (a new security issue date, say) actual market impacts may be quite large. Escaping the Scylla of logical fallacy exposes the theory to the danger of being trapped on the Charybdis of empirical irrelevance.

Provided investment projects satisfied *only* the condition of *economic independence,* they could be valued, the standard theory claimed, as separate entities by the asset market. But this implies that the ownership rights to the project are in fact saleable in the asset market, or that it is separable from the firm of which, at the decision making stage, it is a part. But again questions of logic and empirical relevance arise, for if the project is so small as to have significance for the market price of risk, then conceivably it is so small that it cannot be separately marketed.

What cannot be ignored in the interest of results-by-convenient-assumption is the question of what exactly *is* made available by the corporate sector as financial assets. The XYZ corporation which invests in a new $100 million facility does not in general market the ownership rights or the senior debt securities identifiable with that facility. In the general case, new investment simply influences the structure and activities and income-generating prospects of the existing firm as a whole. It therefore affects the assigned probability description in terms of which, for the equilibrium model, the securities of that firm are regarded in the market. If an automobile manufacturer, for example, undertakes investment of a "cost reducing" kind or invests in order to effect a technological change to implement, say, a new method of making transmissions or pressing automobile bodies, it is surely unreasonable to imagine that such a "project entity" is valued independently in the asset market in the way the standard theory has proposed. Similarly, the financial asset market does not deal in security rights to the product divisions or activity centers of firms, but in the capital securities of firms as a whole.

Cases in which the economic independence assumption is applicable constitute very much the exceptions rather than the general rule in industrial affairs. The evasion of the force of this fact leads to an excessively narrow focus on individual investment project evaluation, to the neglect of larger considerations of the effect of alternative investment options on the profile and prospects of the firm as a whole.[13] This also makes it impossible to regard an industrial firm merely as a

[13]Cf. the two widely used texts by Harold Bierman and Seymour Schmidt, *The Capital Budgeting Decision, Economic Analysis and Financing of Investment Projects,* 2d ed. (New York: Macmillan, 1966), and A. J. Merret and Allen Sykes, *The Finance and Analysis of Capital Projects* (New York: Wiley, 1963), and observe the preoccupation of each with individual project analysis.

portfolio of physical assets to which, for decision purposes, the portfolio asset selection technique can be applied. A firm's investment in *real* capital assets does *not* provide a usable analogue in this sense with *financial* portfolio assets, for it is not possible to specify, in the manner which would be necessary for portfolio theoretic purposes, a permanently separable, specifiable, and probabilistically describable income stream for each project.

This difficulty, of course, confirms rather than vitiates the logic of valuing an incremental investment project by comparing the proposed capital outlay with the future *net incremental cash flow* that may be properly attributed to the project. Leaving aside the computational methods, the marginal cash flow attributable to an investment project must be calculated as the incremental cash flow generated *by the firm as a whole* if the contemplated project is adopted. But while it is true that for optimum decision making at the margin we get at a marginal profitability criterion in this way, it is not possible to treat all of a firm's real assets as marginal investments without pausing to ask what it is to which they are understood to be marginal. And the asking and answering of this question supports our insistence on the evaluation of the firm, and therefore of its outstanding capital securities, as a whole and at specific points in time.

Similar considerations bear also on the covariance term in the investment criterion in Inequality (42). If it is impossible to identify separably the ownership rights to an individual investment project, then it is difficult to regard as meaningful any estimate of the covariance between the cash flow generated by the project and the rate of return on the market portfolio. Again, therefore, the meaning and the empirical viability of this equilibrium theory investment criterion is seriously suspect.

The theoretical development we have had under review in this chapter assumes that no imperfections exist in the financial asset market.[14] But in general, market imperfections—for example, differences between individual investors' borrowing and lending rates, transactions costs, security issue costs, and costs of generating and transmitting information—all militate against the uniqueness of the capital market line, the optimum market portfolio of risky assets, and therefore the market price of risk. And if uniqueness at these points collapses, the logical foundations of whatever prescriptions might be assumed to follow from the theory are damagingly undermined.

If, for example, individual investors were required to bear heavy transactions or information costs in order to achieve their optimum

[14]Cf. Haley and Schall, *Theory of Financial Decisions*, chapters 11 and 14.

portfolio diversification, then it might in fact be beneficial from the shareholders' point of view for the firm to undertake merger or diversification activity on the owners' behalf, notwithstanding the previous suggestions to the contrary. Or again, the tidy prescriptions of the theory may be undermined by a so-called "clientele effect," in which certain kinds of investors are attracted to the securities of certain kinds of firms, or to those of specific firms for other than purely economic-financial reasons. It may not in fact be reasonable at all, therefore, to suppose that all financial assets available in the market can be homogenized simply on the basis of the moments of universally agreed, subjectively assigned probability distributions of their returns.

Imperfections in the markets for financial assets do in fact imply that there may exist after all an optimum financing mix and capital structure policy for the firm, and that production, investment, and financing decisions are not separable as might otherwise be supposed. The foundational "separation theorems" might not be relevant after all. Reflection on the possible ramifications of market imperfections led Haley and Schall to conclude with candor, "In our opinion there is no existing procedure or theory that provides the optimal solution to the financing decision; the determination of the proper mix of financing is still primarily a matter for the informed judgment of management," and "in imperfect markets, the arbitraging mechanism is ineffective or non-existent; the firms themselves must attempt to 'package' their cash flow in the best way possible."[15]

It is well to remember that real-world corporate firms *are* managed by managers who embrace and determine their policy behavior against a variety of corporate goals.[16] It would be ironical in the extreme to establish, in the purported interest of viable financing decision rules, a body of theory actually denying to real-world management the discretion and judgment, which, in the final analysis, is the thing that motivates and vindicates the development of hopefully meaningful theory.

[15]Ibid., p. 249, 250.

[16]Cf. William J. Baumol, *Business Behavior, Value and Growth* (New York: Macmillan, 1959). Robin Marris, *The Economic Theory of "Managerial" Capitalism* (London: Macmillan, 1964), and Oliver E. Williamson, "Managerial Discretion and Business Behavior," *American Economic Review* 53 (December 1963).

7

False Trading in Non-Tatonnement Markets

We now have before us the essential structure and much of the analytical detail of contemporary financial theory. But throughout the development of it I have noted the neglect of such fundamental issues as true or residual uncertainty and the significance of historic time. This chapter examines the very different perspectives that financial theory provides when these, and the false trading that occurs in fact, are taken more carefully into account.

The phenomenon of uncertainty that inheres in historic time, the uniqueness of decision moments, and the variability of expectations mean that the methodology of equilibrium theory is of questionable significance in explaining the place of financial markets as part of the capitalist process. "No one can deny," Robert Clower has observed,

> that general equilibrium analysis, as presently constituted, is a useful instrument for thinking about abstract economic problems, and this would hardly be so if it did not omit many realistic frills. The danger in using this instrument to think about practical problems is that, having schooled ourselves so thoroughly in the virtues of elegant simplicity, we may refuse to recognize the crucial relevance of complications that do not fit our theoretical preconceptions.[1]

The problem becomes particularly acute "if we adopt the view that states of transactor disequilibrium are, in principle, just as admissible as states of transactor equilibrium . . . and how can we do otherwise?"[2] It is therefore implied that the thing that now needs to be taken into account is what we have referred to as the phenomenon of false trading in the real and the financial markets of the economy. By false trading we refer to the consummation of market transactions at non-

[1]Clower, "The Keynesian Conterrevolution: A Theoretical Appraisal," p. 124.
[2]Ibid., p. 116.

equilibrium prices, with consequent asset price perturbations and income and wealth redistribution effects.

But the use of the language of false trading is making a concession to the conventional theory that should not be allowed to become more than semantic. For the phrase is in danger of suggesting that it is in fact possible to describe an equilibrium state of affairs from which the disequilibrium position is a definable deviation. On the contrary, in the continual flux of economic events through the passing of historic time the transactions that occur cannot in general be related to any equilibrium posture or conjuncture at all. There are invariably too many disturbing forces at work, and too many imponderables bearing on actual states of affairs, for that to be the case. Conventions, we have seen, lend a certain orderedness and stability to economic affairs, but as Keynes has put it, "the practice of calmness and immobility, of certainty and security, suddenly breaks down. New fears and hopes will, without warning, take charge of human conduct. The forces of disillusion may suddenly impose a new conventional basis of valuation."[3]

Equilibrium is not the general condition, and our thought forms should not be oriented upon it. Whichever of all the various meanings of economic equilibrium is invoked, the burden of demonstrating its empirical relevance rests heavily on those who wish to use it. On a simpler and more direct view of the world we observe transactors where they actually are, in the actual economic environment that constitutes the inheritance of their decision moment, and subject to the variety of constraints imposed on their decisions in time. The difficulties in the way of deriving meaningful decision rules from the Walrasian equilibrium capital market theory stem from the fact that we do not live in a Walrasian world, and that the Walrasian auctioneer and "the process of tatonnement with recontracting" are not there to help things along.[4] The world is very much a non-tatonnement world. Rigidities, inelasticities, market imperfections, volatile expectations, weaknesses in information transmissions, and the sheer changes of fashion that lend excitement to economic life, keep on getting in the way of simple rules of action.

Against this realization, our objectives in this chapter will be determined by the following propositions. First, it is not coherently possible to construct a theory of financial asset prices without taking account of the interactions with the financial markets of what is transpiring in the underlying real markets of the economy. It is an evasion to propose a theory of financial market equilibrium "conditioned on an assumed equilibrium in the markets for labor and consumption

[3]Keynes, "General Theory of Employment" p. 215.
[4]Fama and Miller, *The Theory of Finance*, p. 278.

goods," or a theory that "examine[s] the characteristics of capital market equilibrium, given a general equilibrium, that is, simultaneous equilibrium in all markets."[5] Too many lines of interconnection between the real and the financial markets exist for this to be a meaningful procedure.

Second, from the temporal (as distinct from timeless) perspective, false trading in the real markets is pervasive. Third, market outcomes in the real sector, along with transactors' dispositions and expectations generated by them, create the information transmitted from the real to the financial markets. This information is seldom "equilibrium" information, and in the general case will not be describable in such terms. The transmission of information affects the structure of trading in the financial markets, including the effects induced by variations in wealth and asset value endowments; and the so-called "efficiency" of the financial markets will therefore need careful interpretation.

Fourth, the forces at work will determine a structure of financial asset market prices at which, on a given day, the market will clear. But it is necessary to keep distinct the concept of "market clearing" outcomes on the one hand and "equilibrium" outcomes on the other. As time does not stand still, market clearing outcomes do not always, or for very long, leave transactors as willing holders of their acquired portfolio positions. Market transactions are always *constrained* transactions, wealth-constrained and knowledge-constrained as well as taste-constrained, and the structures of false trading imply that the constraints themselves will be undergoing change.

Fifth, because of the possibility and even the pervasiveness of false trading in the financial as well as the real markets, the asset price and the effective yield outcomes in turn have crucial significance for decisions and transactions in the real markets of the system. Price and yield outcomes in the financial markets establish criteria for action in the real sector in connection, for example, with a firm's marginal investment expenditure decision.

Finally, the penumbra of uncertainty that surrounds both the real and the financial markets is such that it renders of dubious value the notion that decision making can be adequately subsumed under categories of subjectively assessable risk.

Tatonnement Equilibration

In commodity market models equilibrium was attained, as Walras put it, "*par tatonnement.*"[6] By means of the auctioneer's "groping" pro-

[5]Ibid., p. 279n.

[6]Walras, *Elements of Pure Economics*, pp. 170, 520. Cf. the discussion in Stigler, *Production and Distribution Theories* pp. 244f.

cess, "the upward and downward movement of prices solve the system of equations of offer and demand."[7] By the Walrasian device of "ignoring the time element," or, as Edgeworth supposed, by a process of "recontracting," no transactions actually occurred until a notionally consistent set of equilibrium prices had been determined.[8] It is this same supposition that describes the market equilibrating process in the conventional theory of financial markets also: "Prices and decisions are tentative; it is agreed that no decisions are executed until an equilibrium set of prices . . . has been determined."[9]

Underlying the "pure exchange" form of the Walrasian theory is the assumption that transactors come to the market and enter the tatonnement process with specified endowments of commodities, with endowments of "productive services" again posited in the Walrasian production model.[10] A parallel givenness of an "endowment vector" is imported similarly into the neo-Walrasian financial market theory.[11] Mossin describes the wealth endowments of investors as simply "the total amount of money they want to spend."[12]

The actual working out of the final vector of prices follows from the auctioneer's "price calling" procedure and the market participants' tentative "recontracting." What is not clear in all formulations of the analysis is the interpretation of the givenness of the endowments with which transactors enter the market. Robert Clower has stressed the fact that in *actual* markets the *value* of the transactors' endowments *in an expectational sense* may diverge markedly from the value those endowments acquire *in actual fact*. For example, suppliers of labor, who are potentially income receivers and income spenders, may formulate *notional* demand functions for the commodities they would demand if they were in fact able to sell their available labor services at expected or hoped-for prices. But, in the outcome, the demand for their labor services may be lower than they had anticipated, their incomes will accordingly be lower, and their consumption expenditures will be "constrained" by the lower realized incomes rather than determined by the initial notional demand relations.

Thus the Walrasian excess demand functions are *not* to be under-

[7]Walras, *Elements of Pure Economics*, p. 170.

[8]Ibid., p. 242; cf. Stigler, *Production and Distribution Theories*, pp. 244ff.; see F. Y. Edgeworth, *Papers Relating to Political Economy* (London: Macmillan, 1925), pp. 311, 318, 369.

[9]Fama and Miller, *Theory of Finance*, p. 278. See also the discussion in Kenneth J. Arrow and F. H. Hahn, *General Competitive Analysis* (San Francisco: Holden-Day, 1971), pp. 264ff.

[10]Cf. Walras, *Elements of Pure Economics*, p. 164, on "The general formula of the mathematical solution of the problem of exchange . . . ," and p. 242.

[11]Hirshleifer, *Investment, Interest and Capital*, p. 33 and passim.

[12]Mossin, *Security Pricing Theory*, p. 2.

stood simply as functions of *equilibrium* price vectors. Rather, they are properly definable over *realized* income or endowment arguments also. Demands in one market may be constrained by actually realized results of transactions in other markets. But this shifts the argument from the timeless relationship, which the equilibrium theory has in view, to the transactions that occur in sequences in actual time.

Clower, however, offers the conclusion that to "distinguish between planned and realized magnitudes . . . would not in fact have been a meaningful procedure in the context of orthodox equilibrium analysis;" and he bases this observation on the view that in the "more usual general equilibrium models . . . *current* incomes never appear as independent variables."[13]

In an attempt to circumvent the tatonnement dilemma, Victoria Chick has assumed that each transactor generates a *different* set of excess supply and demand functions for each *different* supposition regarding the income that might be realized from whatever it is that he places on the market. Thus it is misleading, she argues, to imply "that the Walrasian functions are not constrained."[14] On this view it follows that "the constraint varies with the prices cried by the auctioneer. Thus there *are* 'income effects' during the tatonnement approach to equilibrium . . . for the equilibrium price vector itself depends on plans formulated with respect to this *variable budget constraint.*"[15] It follows, then, that it is necessary to take into account the manner in which transactions in given markets will be constrained by realized outcomes in other markets.

Distilling the essential point of the tatonnement controversy, namely the need to be alert to the variations in market behavior in one sector that can result from price, income, or quantity constraint conditions emanating from other sectors, a larger cloud menaces the equilibrium view of the events that work themselves out in economic time. Consider Victoria Chick's argument that *within the Walrasian tatonnement process* there may be a "variable budget constraint." To use such a supposition as a basis for a conclusion regarding the extent to which, for example, Keynes did or did not really present equilibrium or disequilibrium economics is beside the point. Our extensive argument about the uniqueness of decision moments in time implies that all the world of difference attaches to "disequilibrium" transactions and "false trading" which occur in actual historic time, and those

[13]Clower, "The Keynesian Counterrevolution," p. 115, my italics.

[14]Chick, "The Nature of the Keynesian Revolution," forthcoming.

[15]Ibid., my italics. For a further discussion of the lines of analysis opened up by Clower's seminal contribution to the interpretation of Keynesian disequilibrium, see Henri R. Lorie, "A Model of Keynesian Dynamics," forthcoming in *Oxford Economic Papers*.

that might be conceptualized as notionally or potentially occurring in a nontransacting tatonnement process. Occurrences in actual time influence beyond recall transactors' and market participants' "inheritances," wealth endowments, knowledge, and their decision milieu in general.

It is in these latter respects that market transactions in nonequilibrium false trading conjunctures have decided significance for the theory of financial markets, beyond what could be captured by the timeless and static conventional theory.

False Trading

"Production," Walras acknowledged, "requires a certain lapse of time." But it was here that he made his heroic and stultifying assumption: "We shall resolve the . . . difficulty purely and simply by ignoring the time element at this point."[16] The fact that production takes time means that in general commitments to capital budgets and operating costs will be made in advance of the receipt of sales revenue from the marketing of output. The impact of economic time comes formidably into the picture for the firm and for the economy.

The temporal nature of the production process means that businessmen's estimates of operating results, their choices of alternative economic actions, and their best guesses as to outcomes under possible changes in the economic environment, impart incalculable uncertainties to the decision and management process. In the very nature of events there would appear to be every reason why false trading and false production should permeate the enterprise system. Reflection on the earlier argument in Chapter 2 surrounding output, pricing, and standard unit profit calculations and decisions will confirm that in the presence of fluctuations of demand, or in the event that attainable production levels exceed or fall short of standard volume, the firm will actually earn a higher or lower rate of return on its capital employed. A higher than target rate of return that was expected to be permanent would trigger incremental capital investment expenditure in the firm, and a lower than expected return would point to the reallocation of capital resources.

This could precipitate new confrontations between the firm and the money capital or financial asset market, depending on the firm's internally generated cash flow and the management's policy regarding dividend distribution to the stockholders. New issues of capital securities may have to be made, with implications for conditions in the financial

[16]Walras, *Elements of Pure Economics*, p. 242.

asset market. Adequate scope exists for miscalculations, false starts, changes of policy, false trading, and the transmission of false signals from the firms to the rest of the economy, including the financial markets.

At the same time consumers, in their capacity as suppliers of labor, will be estimating their incomes from employment in the time period immediately ahead and will make plans for consumption expenditures. The demand for labor will follow from the producers' decisions as to their standard volume of operation and may or may not result in an excess supply or a deficiency of demand for labor. In estimating sales, incomes, employment, and expenditures, decision makers on all sides of the market may expect the previously prevailing conditions to continue, bringing to concrete expression Keynes's reliance on "conventions," although, as we have seen, conventions may change rapidly and with minimal warning.

If the demand for labor should fall, wage earners' actual incomes may be below their notional or expected incomes, and their consumption expenditure plans will be revised downwards. Thus expenditures in the consumer goods markets can become unexpectedly constrained by actual income receipts. In the meantime, as output flows onto the markets the sellers' income expectations will either be fulfilled or falsified. If the firms' expectations are falsified, production plans may be modified in either direction, implying a reduction or acceleration of incremental investment expenditures. If firms' expectations are fulfilled, even though unemployment exists, the production cycle may well be repeated and a condition of underemployment equilibrium may obtain.

Induced changes may occur at any time in the supply of labor, labor force participation rates may change, and wage aspirations and expectations may vary. Much will depend again on conventions and on the possible elasticity of expectations. As part of the determinants of the environment or "inheritance" in which the process is going on, changes may be induced in monetary, fiscal, or other government economic policies. Included in initial expectations also are projected savings rates by income recipients, as well as savings from allocations of corporate cash flows. Again a good deal of room exists for miscalculation, misjudgment, false signals, and false trading.

False trading occurs because decisions have to be made and *are* made at specific points in time, and no Edgeworthian "recontracting" enters the picture. When in conditions of even minor eruptions in both real and financial markets speculative activity also enters, further scope for false signals, false decisions, and false trading is provided. Induced changes in time preferences may occur, with impact effects on financial markets and the flow of funds. Speculation may ultimately be stabilizing in its price or output effects, but it can exploit the disequilibrium moment, however well or badly it shares in the formation of underlying market trends.

Even this brief look at the scope for false trading carries us a long way from the Walrasian general equilibrium abstractions. Contemplating these issues, Clower concluded that "either Walras' Law is incompatible with Keynesian economics, or Keynes had nothing fundamentally new to add to orthodox economic theory."[17] It is remarkable that the theory of the financial markets should have consolidated its commitment to neoclassical Walrasian postulates of market perfection when skepticism of them has become widespread in other parts of economic theory. In the areas of money, production, capital, labor markets, and distribution there has been an assault and some cracking of the crust of orthodoxy, even, some would say, the crumbling of the orthodox citadel.[18] But the theory of financial markets and the financial theory of the firm have remained deeply committed to the neo-Walrasian, neoclassical orthodoxy.

False Trading and the Asset Market Model

In approaching the implications of false trading for the principal result of the equilibrium market model we recall the conclusion:

$$E(R_j) = R_F + \beta_j[E(R_M) - R_F]. \tag{1}$$

We shall understand $E(R_j)$ in this equation to describe the market's equilibrium required rate of return on the *j*th firm's common stock. $E(R_M)$ and R_F represent respectively the expected return on the market portfolio and the rate of return on a risk-free asset, or the risk-free rate of interest. β_j again reflects the systematic risk of the asset, or $\beta_j = \text{Cov}(R_j, R_M)/\text{Var}(R_M)$.

To what extent, we can now ask, will the specification of the required rate of return in Equation (1) be meaningfully usable as a financing and investment decision criterion in the real-world corporate firm? We can remind ourselves of the point that even if historically observable data led us to place credence in the Equation (1) relationship, the firm would still need for use as an economic decision criterion a best estimate of the *future* relationship that could be expected to obtain. Here the inductive leap that bedevils the logical positivist bequest to our discipline raises its head, raising the question

[17]Clower, "The Keynesian Counterrevolution," p. 110.

[18]Cf. the valuable and important surveys of modern theory in Davidson, *Money and the Real World*, and Weintraub, *Modern Economic Thought*.

of the extent to which tomorrow will really be describable in the same way as yesterday. The problem exists because the human and social sciences are concerned with thinking, sentient, acting beings, and with their imaginations and endeavors. Shackle has observed that "it is not even the lack of exactness in its measurements . . . but the extent to which their subject matter consists of *thoughts* and not of *objects*, which makes the assimilation of economic analysis to mechanical science dangerous."[19]

Our argument may well raise the impression that if we delete from financial theory the assumptions of Walrasian tatonnement, Edgeworthian recontracting, market perfection, and infinite price adjustment velocities, then we are left without the ability to erect a general equilibrium theory at all, and economic theory is on that account so much the poorer. We respect the inference but deny the implication, for any appearance of logical generality possessed by contemporary asset market theory is, by virtue of its evasion of disequilibrium forces, spurious at its best. Moreover, relinquishing a preoccupation with general equilibrium analysis in no sense implies that economic theory is thereby the poorer. New horizons of more serious empirical relevance will be discovered if the constraints of equilibrium thought forms are vacated.

We can raise explicitly, therefore, the question of the dependence that can be placed on the stability over time, and over varying conditions in the real markets in the economy, of the $E(R_j)$ in Equation (1). This, it can be seen, turns on the stability of the risk-free rate of interest in differing economic conjunctures, on the overall market risk premium or the market price of risk, and on the responsiveness of the return on the security of firm j to changes in the overall market return.

Variations in real market output volumes, prices, and trading activity raise the likelihood of changes in wealth endowments emanating from that source, changes in expectations, variations in real asset and liquidity demands, disturbances in financial market conditions and in money demand and supplies, and therefore changes in R_F, the risk-free rate of interest. If decisions should be made to undertake additional money capital investment, the resulting finance motive demand for money will reinforce other pressures to an upward movement in the general structure of interest rates.[20]

In this connection we can invoke again the Keynesian proposition that in the context of changing supplies and demands in the money markets, there may nevertheless exist conventions on what the short-

[19]Shackle, *Epistemics & Economics*, p. 66, italics in original. Cf. also the extensive discussion of positivist epistemology in Hollis and Nell, *Rational Economic Man*.

[20]Cf. Davidson, *Money and the Real World*, chapter 7.

and the long-term rates of interest should be. Deviations from conventionally established norms will be likely to set in motion speculative forces that will react back on the level and the stability of the market rates. But of course the picture changes, and variations in real economic activity can dislodge the yield curve which shows the established pattern of short- and long-term rates. Normally, because conventions tend more firmly to govern long-term attitudes, the short-term rates exhibit the more pronounced changes during cyclical business fluctuations.

Variations in the Keynesian speculative demand for money involve forces that are in no sense captured in the assumed portfolio theoretic explanation of a smooth southeast-sloping demand for money curve. We have seen that Tobin's probability argument and portfolio analysis leave quite untouched the Keynesian speculative dimension. We have noted also Keynes's own denial that the liquidity preference function could be assumed to be in any sense stable. For our own purposes, then, we must take account of the possible dislodgement of the risk-free interest rate, and its dependence on the elasticity of expectations held by the preponderance of transactors in the market. We must be concerned, that is, with the volatility of the conventions that guide and underpin the market.[21]

Expectations, moreover, enter at several other parts of the analysis also. A deterioration may occur in the state of long-run expectations or in the marginal efficiency of capital. Pessimism in regard to prospective income streams on real capital assets can reduce the economic value of such assets below their current supply price. Investment expenditures in the economy can then be expected to fall, with repercussions through familiar multiplier effects. In such an event, the economic value of real assets could be raised again and a structure of relative prices conducive to a revival of investment could be established, if, when the decline in long-run expectations occurred, a reduction could be effected in the rate of interest.[22] But an inelasticity of expectations in the financial markets may well militate against just that occurrence.

This inelasticity of expectations in the financial sector may then reinforce the possibly cumulative effects of the same kind of inelasticity of expectations in the real markets of the economy. Producers, for

[21]Cf. A. G. Hines, *On the Reappraisal of Keynesian Economics* (London: Martin Robinson, 1971), pp. 30-31.

[22]Though it is beyond our immediate line of analysis it is apposite to observe that this matter of the Keynesian importance of *relative* prices, the prices of real capital goods relative to consumer goods, is missed completely by a monetary analysis anchored solely to a quantity theory of money or the concept of a homogeneous price level or a single sector aggregate model.

example, may hold inelastic expectations as to viable commodity price levels, and this may diminish the adjustment of prices in a cumulative downward movement and may produce instead an implicitly higher quantity adjustment velocity. Involved also may be an inelasticity of expectations regarding viable factor prices (for example, the expectation of wage rates), which may lead again to widening unemployment rather than to the neoclassical automatic equilibration of the labor market at full employment wage and employment levels.

In the course of such cumulative movements the question of the achievement of a Walrasian generalized equilibrium will have become quite irrelevant. Markets do not automatically clear at Walrasian equilibrium price and quantity vectors at all. False trading becomes pervasive, and there is no Walrasian auctioneer to help things along. Transactors have to learn from the progressive falsification of their expectations. They learn by doing. There are imperfect channels of information transmission, and expectations elasticities have gradually to be adjusted.

Continuing to focus on the equilibrium relation depicted in Equation (1), not only do variations in external economic conjunctures affect in these ways the first term, R_F, on the right-hand side of the equation. They affect also the final bracketed term, or the market price of risk. Any variation in the risk-free rate of interest, the introduction of which into the investors' asset opportunity set permitted the linearization of the efficient investment opportunity locus, will change the slope of the capital market line and the identity of the optimum portfolio of risky assets. Thus we may expect to encounter induced changes in the R_F, the $E(R_M)$ and $\sigma(R_M)$, and the λ market price of risk component of the equilibrium model's principal results.

Important and identifiable economic forces in financial markets are unleashed when expectations are falsified or conventions change. For one thing, realized profits and rentier incomes in the real sector directly influence the wealth endowments of investors in the financial asset markets and modify their optimum portfolio strategy. Also, variations in interest rates generate a portfolio wealth effect directly altering transactor endowments. We are a long way, that is to say, from the basic postulate of the equilibrium market theory that assumes, for purposes of determining the equilibrium asset price vector, that transactor endowments are given and fixed.

In the same way as imperfections in information transmission inhibit equilibration in real markets, similarly erroneous signals in the financial markets have comparable implications for false trading. Information entering the financial market may be rapidly assimilated there and reflected in asset prices. But information of poor quality, inconsistent with imagined Walrasian equilibrating conditions, can precipitate disorder before some kind of equilibrium in the Robinsonian sense of the fulfillment of expectations is achieved.[23]

False trading can thus occur at a number of points in the economic and financial system. The financial markets themselves, moreover, might not be as efficient in the information transmission sense as has been supposed. For information, knowledge, and the discovery and transmission of it is not cost-free. Indeed, in both the real and the financial market environments, "perfect" information is unattainable. Not only would this involve "knowing" tomorrow, but if full and complete information were achieved the marginal value productivity of it would be driven to zero. But as the information-gathering and dissemination process is costly, presumably the amount and quality of information available will accord with marginal optimization principles, such that the presumed marginal value of it will be no less than the marginal cost of acquiring it. Clearly, the prevalence of false signals in the asset markets as in the real markets confounds the foresight assumptions of the general equilibrium models.

The realism of the multimarket system impinges further on the final term in Equation (1), or on the determination of the market price of risk. First, wealth-induced variations in utility functional forms may occur, and the investor's marginal rate of substitution between risk and return may be dependent on wealth levels or variations in wealth endowments. This in turn may have implications for asset market outcomes if the assumption of homogeneous expectations is relaxed, for in the case of heterogeneous expectations the full description of the theoretical equilibrium conditions involves combinations of individual investors' marginal rates of substitution between risk and return, and it is not possible to eliminate utility information to obtain equilibrium relationships stated solely in terms of observable market parameters.[24]

Furthermore, disequilibrium developments and false trading in the real markets transmit to the financial markets effects on the subjectively assigned probability distributions of the various assets' returns and the projected covariances between them. In the probabilistic specification of the asset opportunity set, their influence will extend to the location and the form of the efficient boundary of that set. To the extent that this occurs, the location and slope of the capital market line is affected, the equilibrium market price of risk is varied, and the price

[23]Cf. Robinson, "The Production Function and the Theory of Capital," and the discussion in Harcourt, *Some Cambridge Controversies in the Theory of Capital*, p. 22.

[24]Cf. the discussion of this point in the work of John Lintner and Michael C. Jensen, previously cited.

and yield vectors implicit in the market portfolio are affected as a result. Thus two reasons for variation in the actual and effective market price of risk inherent in Equation (1) emerge. First, the risk-free rate of interest to which the presumed capital market line is anchored at one end may be unstable; and second, instabilities may reside in the risky asset efficient set boundary that anchors the capital market line at the other end.

Against the "pure exchange" model's assumption of a *given* quantity of securities or a given opportunity set, the false trading developments can cause additions to or deletions from this set. Firms go out of operation, or change their commodity production and therefore their real market orientations, while new firms emerge as the economy moves onward in time. But such variations and commonplace events are unfortunately not accommodated in the static exchange model assumptions. Fama and Miller recognize the issue, but they invoke the "assumption that the firm's production decisions *do not affect the equilibrium picture of the efficient set.* If the firm's activities affect the combinations of $E(R)$ and $\sigma(R)$ that are available in equilibrium, it affects its shareholders' expected utilities by its effects on their . . . wealth levels and on the portfolio opportunity set."[25] The equilibrium model takes care of its most difficult problems by assuming them away, and the analysis does not accommodate to the realities of the economic history of the capitalist process.

The condition specified in Equation (1) requires a consideration also of the stability or instability of the *j*th firm's beta coefficient. We are alerted to the possible causes of instability by the realization that the empirical analogue of this variable is the regression coefficient of the firm's rate of return on the return realized by the total market portfolio of securities. Stability in such a relationship may appear to provide a reasonably sure foundation for predictive purposes. But the logical distinction between prediction and explanation must be borne in mind, and the espousal of methodological positivism acknowledged.[26] Whatever might have been the stability of the coefficient in the past, it can for a number of reasons change in the future.

Even if there is no change in the internal structure of the firm, nevertheless in a non-Walrasian, non-market-clearing economy the achieved correlation between different economic transactors' realized results, of income and wealth, could vary. The multitudinous causes

[25]Fama and Miller, *Theory of Finance*, pp. 300-301, my italics.

[26]I shall not discuss the applicability of Hines' complaint, in the context of a different aspect of neoclassical economics, that "we have been asked to accept the rather dubious positivist principle that the sole relevant test of a theory is its ability to predict much from little," *Reappraisal*, p. 33.

pointing in this direction are implicit in our earlier disequilibrium argument. The magnitude and stability of the beta coefficient will depend also on the internal structure of the firm, and on possible changes in that structure resulting from new investment and new capital financing.

The determinants of the stability or otherwise of the firm's residual equity income stream have already been discussed at length in many places.[27] The firm's interdependent production, investment, and financing decisions determine the optimum size and structure of its operations and the optimum structure of money capital sources by which it is financed. In terms more familiar to business literature, they determine its optimum "operational leverage" on the one hand and its optimum "financial leverage" on the other. Taking note of the possible use in the firm of more or less capital-intensive production methods, and thereby of the relative importance of fixed and variable operating costs, implications prevail for the stability of the residual earnings stream and therefore of the firm's beta coefficient.

By effecting changes in any of these structural determinants, the earnings stability, and the nature of the uncertainty surrounding it, can be projected into the future. Including, as these determinants do, the question of the factor combination in the firm and its degree of real capital intensity, any attempt to rescue the more direct applicability of the asset market equilibrium condition by assuming the factor mix problem away would seem to be self-defeating. Fama and Miller, for example, embrace the assumption that the "firm is in a given risk class, and its only decision is to choose the optimum scale of activity."[28] The critical factor proportions problem has not come into focus at all.

This assumption, that real investment activities are scale-changing, risk-class-preserving investments only, is similar to that of the Modigliani and Miller analysis. Attempts have been made to generalize the investment decision criterion away from this essentially nondiversifying activity. But in general the factor proportions problem has not been integrated explicitly into the analysis. Mossin, for example, has endeavored to show that the properties of the general equilibrium capital market model can be used to specify an investment decision criterion for any marginal investment, whatever its kind.[29] But unfortunately, the premises of the argument appear to render it quite unus-

[27]See Vickers, *Theory of the Firm*, and "The Cost of Capital and the Structure of the Firm."

[28]Fama and Miller, *Theory of Finance*, p. 311n., cf. pp. 301-2 and p. 299.

[29]Mossin, *Security Pricing Theory*, pp. 14ff. See also the same author's *Theory of Financial Markets*, chapter 7, pp. 124ff.

able, for it assumes that a covariance matrix can be defined, specifying not only the covariance relationship between the income stream of the existing firm and that of its proposed marginal investment, but also the covariances between the marginal project of that firm and the earnings streams of all other firms in the investors' opportunity set. It is questionable that a firm's individual investment projects are in this way empirically and permanently separable and preservable as independently viable economic entities.

Moreover, the Mossin formulation involves also the explicit "assumption that the market risk-aversion factor will not change as a result of the investment." Yet it may in fact change, as Mossin acknowledges, for at "generally different levels of wealth . . . risk-aversion varies with the level of return," but "we can . . . treat this change as a minor second-order effect by assuming that the number of firms is so large that a change in the return in any one of them does not appreciably affect the market risk-aversion factor."[30] But it does not seem that the problem can be assumed away as easily as that. In real-world aggregative disequilibrium structures, the capital market is likely to be confronted not only with such minimal second-order effects as these. Real investment variations and capital market changes are likely, for the reasons we have examined, to be of much larger orders of magnitude.

The Cost of Capital and Investment Criteria

It follows that the suggestion of the asset market theory that Equation (1) provides a cost of capital datum usable as an investment decision criterion is hardly applicable to real-world firms. Similarly, the firm's investment decision criterion in Inequality (42) of the preceding chapter, derived from the equilibrium conditions of the financial asset market model, is subject to all of the criticisms, difficulties, and disadvantages of that model which have been examined in this chapter. It may appear that our direct approach to the full marginal cost of relaxing the money capital availability constraint as a decision criterion, rather than acquiescing in the market equilibrium condition, is a retreat from recent analytical advances. This, however, is not so, for our importation into financial theory of the implications of market disequilibria and constrained solution outcomes means that no single historically generated datum, such as the capital market model provides, could be employed for economic decision making purposes without a very full adjustment for changes in the forces determining it.

[30]Mossin, *Security Pricing Theory*, p. 15.

The same rigorous and burdensome demands are imposed on decision making by the interdependence of forces within the firm and by the relaxation of constraints which we have called for.

Eschewing the simplicities of historically generated equilibrium market formulas, we have imposed on managements the need for hard empirical judgments regarding the extent to which, if the firm increases its use of debt financing, for example, it can expect increases in both its debt and equity costs of capital. The need exists for careful and responsible judgment of the likely magnitudes of $\Delta r/\Delta D$ and $\Delta\rho/\Delta D$ as debt capital financing is increased.

In imperfect market environments, in structurally disequilibrium situations, in conditions of residual or Knightian or Keynesian uncertainties that cannot be probabilistically reduced to risk and provide certainty equivalents, decision makers have to judge what rates of return can be expected on money capital investments, what risks are involved, how the risk-averting suppliers of money capital can be expected to react to unfolding situations, and what, in light of answers to these questions, are deemed to be economically viable or optimum courses of action. No doubt these are part of the reason why Keynes spoke so much of "animal spirits" when it came to investment decisions in the economy, and why he was so concerned with residual uncertainty and entrepreneurial responsibility in relation to it.

III

Decisions Under Uncertainty: A Nondistributional Variable Approach

8

Possibility, Surprise, and the Decision Function

The foundations for this and the following chapter have been laid in discussions of uncertainty, historic time, and the uniqueness of the decision maker's inheritance and his decision moment. These have led to an examination of the disequilibrium developments in actual markets and the step-by-step changes that occur in them. The question now before us concerns the extent to which the variables that influence decisions can be understood as distributional variables, or as describable by objectively given or subjectively assigned probability distributions.

I argue that in the general case, certainly in the case of capital investment expenditures, the variables are not distributional variables at all, and that the familiar probability calculus cannot therefore be applied to them. In the uncertainties in which real-world decisions are enmeshed, some viable procedure for coming to grips with decision responsibility is required, and my objective will be that of developing an alternative nondistributional variable approach. In doing so we shall import into financial theory something of the remarkable insight available in the work of Shackle, who has written extensively in related areas and whose contributions can be inspected in a number of sources.[1] In what follows we shall endeavor to take those initial steps in what, it is to be hoped, will in due course become a larger body of newly oriented financial and economic theory.

The essential and troublesome question remains that of the meaning and treatment of uncertainty. The matter at issue is not simply uncertainty as distinct from risk. It is grounded in the fact that the

[1]I refer in particular to Shackle's recent volumes, in which he has reexamined and brought up to date his important contributions to economic theory, *Decision, Order, and Time* and *Epistemics & Economics*.

human perception of ***uncertainty*** is bound up with the perception of the fact and the significance of ***time***. The fact that economic decisions are always decisions in time, temporally bounded and having temporal referents, introduces the rigor and the challenges to our problem. The bequest to economics of positivist methodology has substantially elided the complexities of time by encouraging the conception that our vision of tomorrow can be safely delimited by our knowledge of yesterday.

Neoclassical theory, it can be said, is "a story in logical time," and the difficulties that inhere in its practical application derive from the inductive leap, the epistemological hiatus, in the problems that arise in predicting tomorrow from our ordering of our knowledge of yesterday.[2] "A prediction model is supposed to generate conclusions in *historical* time from a theory operating in *logical* time."[3] There is a logically inescapable human drama even in simple economic activities, such as occurs in the Hollis and Nell parable of buying shoes. There,

> all its dithering and indecision is finally reduced to the variable 'quantity of shoes.' The relations of this variable to others are those and only those specified in the model. But in reality we may forget, change our minds, develop a craze for bare feet, in the middle of carrying out our normal pattern of purchases. History is open. . . . Our actual economic activities . . . take time.[4]

And,

> neo-Classical time is a sort of logical abstraction, where each position on a supply or demand curve has its own infinite past and future and represents a hypothetical fully adjusted ***equilibrium situation***. There is no *movement* from point to point on a neo-Classical curve. There is only a hypothetical *comparison* of what might have been. . . . But actual events occur in historical, not in logical, time . . . creating real constraints.[5]

It is apposite to acknowledge that "positivism has no epistemological basis for induction."[6] Consider our present question of the explanatory efficiency and usefulness of the calculus of probability. We can acknowledge the positivist tenets that all cognitively meaningful statements are either analytic or synthetic. The former, being true by convention, are devoid of factual content, and the latter, being refutable on the basis of experience, cannot be known to be true *a priori*. It follows, then, that possible "scientific" status adheres, on these

[2]Hollis and Nell, *Rational Economic Man*, p. 183.
[3]Ibid., p. 183, my italics.
[4]Ibid., p. 183.
[5]Ibid., p. 227, italics partially supplied.
[6]Ibid., p. 199.

grounds, only to synthetic propositions or hypotheses. But when we consider in this light the question of probability, with the riddle of induction hanging tenaciously to it, it is necessary to recognize that statements of probability are all too frequently not synthetic statements at all, or statements whose truth content is subject to empirical test. In general they are analytic statements in a thin synthetic disguise. To the extent that this is so, the imagined "scientific" status of the probability statements evaporates. Unfortunately for those who would rely on a probabilistic understanding of things in economics, analyticity is immune to empirical refutation. For "even if the sun fails to rise tomorrow, it remains true that it was likely that it would."[7] This is the nature of the position we are in when economic outcome variables are assumed to be probabilistically described. The nature of the inductive problem that underlies the probability calculus is only worsened in economics, where the problems demanding attention are inevitably wrapped up with time, with the passage of time, and with the fact that, as Shackle has put it, "economics is concerned with *thoughts about things*" and not simply with objects or things themselves.[8]

Shackle has placed the economic decision maker in his "solitary moment" by saying that "at the moment when the decision maker is free to choose between acts, and still able to create for them fresh imagined outcomes, the future, which will be partly created by this choice and a million similar contemporary ones made by other decision makers, does not yet exist."[9] "There is" he has said, "no objective future," and economic choices are not choices among objectively available things at all.[10] It is true that "economics is about choice, but choice is amongst pure creations of the mind. . . ."[11] "The outcomes by comparison of which an act is chosen from amongst rival acts must be *imagined* outcomes. . . . Choice amongst outcomes takes place in the individual's imagination. . . . Outcomes are figments and imaginations. This idea and its implications lie at the root of our argument."[12]

In saying that there is no objective future, we are locking the decision maker into his solitary decision moment and acknowledging that so far as the specification of outcomes is concerned there is "no attainable future, outside our own minds, with which we can have any

[7]Ibid., p. 76.
[8]Shackle, *Epistemics & Economics*, p. xviii.
[9]Shackle, *Decision, Order and Time*, p. 9.
[10]Ibid., p. 15.
[11]Shackle, *Epistemics & Economics*, p. 74.
[12]Shackle, *Decision, Order, and Time*, p. 9.

contact whatever. All that is, is in the present. . . . The future is not there to be discovered, but must be created."[13]

But to conceive in this way of the present is to allow the notion of economic time to throw its full light on what is meant by economic decision, for in the present all exists. "The past exists in memory, but memory is a mental act of the present."[14] Expectation of the future is also present, and "expectation and memory are part of the essence of the moment in being."[15] While records of the past exist (statistical records perhaps), including, to recall the earlier discussion in Part II, those of the historically generated covariances between a risky asset's periodic rate of return and the rate of return earned on a market portfolio, nevertheless those records exist in the present and they are consulted in the present. And the point to be noted is that the decision maker's choices that follow from his consultation of those records are always *choices among the alternative constructions of his own imagination* at the moment at which the choice decisions are made.

For reasons such as these Shackle has pressed home the meaning of time and the decision moment by insisting that the decision-choice among available acts is aimed at securing "a preferred combination of experiences," but "experience by imagination"; and the "expectation" on which the choice among imaginations turns is construed as "imagination constrained to congruity with what seems in some degree possible."[16] Indeed, the imagination of what is possible evolves out of one's knowledge of the past, his "inheritance," the existing milieu of action, and the perception of the real time lying ahead within which events will work themselves out.

If legitimacy attaches to our perspective, then so far as the decision maker's evaluation is concerned,

> no statement involving two actualities, that is, actuality at two distinct dates, can have any meaning; for it is a logical self-contradiction, a contradiction in terms. The present moment of actuality, the moment in being, is . . . unique . . . so far as the thoughts and feelings, perceptions, judgments, decisions and actions of the human individual are concerned. Comparison of the individual's *actual* experiences at two distinct moments is impossible and meaningless.[17]

This is not denying the statistical and economic significance of describing successive events in historic time. It is not denying that an outcome at a point in time can be quantitatively compared with what,

[13]Ibid., pp. 15-16.
[14]Ibid., p. 16.
[15]Ibid., p. 40.
[16]Ibid., p. 13.
[17]Ibid., p. 18, italics in original.

at an earlier point in time, was thought might be the outcome. What *is* being said is that an economic observer *at one point in time* cannot meaningfully compare his subjective evaluations of an outcome at *that* point in time with the state of his imaginaion in which, at an *earlier* point in time, he evaluated the *possible* outcomes.

The uniqueness of the unfolding moments in historic time prohibits, for example, the attachment of meaning to the comparison of points on an assumedly stable intertemporal utility function. For time "cannot pass without modifying knowledge."[18] And it is the change, the modification or accretion of knowledge, that prohibits the assumption of the stability in the identity of an economic individual which would make the intertemporal comparison of mental states meaningful.

No meaning can attach, therefore, to a comparison between the utility that is expected *now* to result from an outcome *in the future* and the utility *actually* realized *at the future date* when the outcome actually occurs. The comparisons that *can* be made are confined to the *now*, at the *same* moment at which different possible outcomes are contemplated.

In saying that expectation is imagination constrained to congruity with the possible, we have given point to our principal argument. For we shall be concerned with the decision maker's contemplation of the *possible*, and we can envisage the *potential surprise* he would experience if various *possible* outcomes were to occur. The reorientation of thought patterns now required in financial decision making turns on the understanding of *possibilities* and the degrees of *potential surprise* with which they are contemplated. We shall not, that is to say, speak of *probabilities* at all, and the notion of the efficient assignment of probabilities to alternative outcomes will be avoided completely.

Uncertainty as Probability?

On probability, E. Roy Weintraub, reflecting on Keynes's stand on the matter, concludes:

> Any choice now among future alternatives is thus fundamentally uncertain, since the future is logically unknowable. No sampling from the future is feasible to ascertain probabilities for future alternatives, so there is *no way uncertainty problems can be reduced to problems involving risk.*[19]

[18]Ludwig M. Lachmann, *Metroeconomica*, 11 (1959), quoted in Shackle, *Decision, Order and Time*, p. 41.

[19]E. Roy Weintraub, "'Uncertainty' and the Keynesian Revolution," *History of Political Economy* 7 (1975): 532.

But let it be imagined for the present that a statement of probability is before us. This may be a statement that *in a large number of conceivable experiments* there is well-attested reason to believe that *in a specified proportion of the total number of outcomes* a designatable result will emerge. In this sense *statistical* probabilities have meaning and applicability in economic affairs, in life insurance mortality tables for examples, perhaps in the daily cash flows generated by a firm's repetitive operations, and perhaps to a lesser extent in inventory fluctuations in high turnover commodities. In general the experiments to the outcomes of which probabilities are applied must be seriable, or replicable, and no aspect of uniqueness should surround the experiment to prohibit its recall and subsequent reproduction.

On the other hand, the statement of probability may purport to be a description of the likelihood that *in a single experiment*, or as a result of a *single and unique decision*, a designated possible result will emerge. In *this* sense the statement of probability has no meaning. Suppose a probability statement is made as a result of some calculation. Now,

> as a statement of *probability*, it is more than a mere record of calculation done. It claims not only that a figure . . . has been coherently derived within a calculus but also that what is predicted *is in fact as likely to occur as the figure in theory indicates*. . . . Statistics is a calculus of *probabilities* only insofar as some statement that known correlations are likely to hold in unknown cases is true.[20]

And a statement to the latter effect would be an analytic and not a synthetic statement whose truth content is open to test or refutation.

The assignment of probabilities to *future* possible outcomes, either in the form of assumedly objectively given probability distributions or of subjectively assigned probability distributions, is actually an *assumption of knowledge*. It is this that makes the entire probability machinery inapplicable to decisions under uncertainty, for knowledge is the antithesis of uncertainty; it is the abolition of uncertainty. Thus the assignment of a probability distribution to possible outcomes involves the assertion that if the same event were to be repeated a large number of times, a designatable outcome *would actually emerge* in a pre-specifiable proportion of the instances. This, it can be said, is an *assumption of knowledge* that disqualifies the probability calculus for the tasks we have in view, quite apart, as we have pointed out, from the disqualification that arises from the *uniqueness* of the preponderant number of economic decision situations.

For probabilities to be assigned over a set of possible outcomes, the

[20]Hollis and Nell, *Rational Economic Man*, pp. 75-76, italics partially supplied.

assumption must be made that the set is complete and exhaustively descriptive of the possibilities *without a residual hypothesis.* As a homely example, imagine that of six candidates for a job one is, on all the grounds we can contemplate, the most qualified for the position. We accordingly assign probabilities of success to each of the six candidates with this imagination in mind. The probabilities assigned sum to unity and we have, apparently, a *bona fide* probability distribution of the outcome. Suppose now a seventh candidate is introduced, and that he appears to possess much the same qualifications as five of the six previous candidates. Now when we introduce the seventh individual to the candidate set we can assign a probability distribution over the seven possible outcomes, and still have the necessary summation of probabilities to unity, only by taking away part of the probabilities already assigned to one or more of the other six. If, then, we try to capture and corral the uncertainty by treating the outcome variable in this way as a *distributional* variable we are making the assignment of probabilities dependent on the number of possible outcomes in view, even though the very meaning of probability assignment implies the assumption that the distribution encompasses an *exhaustive* specification of the set of possible outcomes.

Shackle has observed that "it is inherent in the use of a distributional uncertainty variable, that if extra hypotheses are each to be accorded non-zero values of the variable, some of the hypotheses in the initial list must be deprived of part of their shares of it."[21] To be forced to conceive of the probability of an outcome as depending on the number of possible outcomes we are able to contemplate is not an efficient or logically sustainable approach to grappling with the uncertainties that inhere in actual affairs. But we can take our example further.

Imagine that one of our original six candidates for the job was, so far as we could see, much superior in qualification to the remaining five. We can ask ourselves then to what extent we would be surprised if that outstanding candidate was awarded the job. With this in mind let us again suppose that the seventh individual possessed qualifications which were comparable with those of the five and were again quite below those of our previous outstanding candidate. We can now ask ourselves the telling question: How surprised would we *now* be if the outstanding man were awarded the job? Would we be less or more surprised than we would have been in the original situation? It may well be the case that the introduction of the seventh candidate makes no difference at all to our contemplation of the outcome so far as the

[21]Shackle, *Decision, Order, and Time,* p. 51.

outstanding candidate is concerned. And in the light of this surely a means of handling uncertainty in decision making situations needs to be devised which can take account of precisely that kind of possibility.

To focus, however, on the conceivable uniqueness of decision situations and decision events, let us ask the following questions by way of illustration. Would it have been meaningful for Napoleon to have assigned a probability distribution to the outcome of the battle of Waterloo? We may answer in the negative on the grounds that if he won the battle there would be no need to repeat it, and if he lost the battle it would not be possible to fight it again. Or to bring the example closer to our field of inquiry, would it have been meaningful to assign a probability distribution to the outcomes of bankruptcy or success of the Penn Central Railroad following the merger that brought it into existence? The outcome is now economic history, and the reader who is familiar with the bankruptcy that resulted can pause and contemplate the interpretation of the expected value and variance of whatever probability distribution might previously have been assigned to the outcome.

In many economic situations, in investment decisions in real-world firms for example, the decision events are unique in the same sense as was Napoleon's situation. And the taking of such business decisions forever changes the decision environment and the decision nexus beyond recall. The uniqueness or the nonrepetitive character of business investment decisions follows from the fact that even though such decisions seemingly recur the decisions themselves are separated in time, frequently by large lengths of time, and they have their own distinctive "inheritance" and milieu. We have already seen the uniqueness inherent in temporally separate moments in economic affairs. Moreover, each investment decision will of necessity envisage a future expected income stream in return for the investment outlay, and it is only in terms of the present discounted values of those income streams that they can be compared. But at any reasonable discount factor the present value of an investment made ten years from now could hardly command a value in current terms which would make it commensurate with current outlays in such a way as to enable it to be pooled in a probability sense to assess its likely success or failure.

For all these reasons, then, we shall replace the concept of probability in what follows by an argument couched in terms of what we shall call a nondistributional outcome variable. We shall proceed by first presenting the essence of the argument and then considering some of the possible objections and misunderstandings to which it might give rise.

Possibility and Surprise

In speaking of possibility and surprise, Shackle has approached the decision making problem from the opposite side from that on which probability thought forms are imagined to be applicable. Instead of asking the decision maker the probability he would assign to a certain specifiable outcome, Shackle envisages him as attaching a measure of *disbelief* to the outcome. We shall imagine that confronted with a range of possible outcomes the decision maker specifies, on an ordinal scale whose units of measurement need not detain us for the present, the degree of *potential surprise* he feels *now*, at the decision moment, he would experience if various outcomes were to occur. By focusing on degrees of disbelief in the description of possible outcomes, our argument will be protected against any attempt to transform it into an argument in probability. The logic of the case is such that *the potential surprise function is in no sense transmutable into a probability density function.* When we speak of the disbelief or the potential surprise with which a decision maker contemplates a possible outcome, we refer to the surprise which, *at the moment of decision*, he *imagines* he would experience if the outcome in view occurred.

But of course the moment in which, in the future, the event that was previously in view *actually* occurs is different from the moment at which the decision is made on the basis of the contemplated *potential* surprise. Our argument on the matter of economic time implies that there is no meaning in the question of what surprise the decision maker *would* get *in the future* if a specified event occurred. He is concerned with the contemplation *now* of the *potential* surprise with which he contemplates the various possible outcomes of his decision.

To give definiteness to these ideas, let us consider the relationship described in Figure 12.[22] The horizontal axis measures the values of an outcome variable X, which we can assume for the present to be money values, thus providing a continuous scale. Outcome values to the right of the zero point are understood to be positive, and those to the left will be negative. The variable X may denote, for example, the present discounted value of the income stream generated by an investment, and the X values distributed around the zero point then

[22]The present exposition draws very heavily on the work of Shackle, which has been presented in a number of forms during recent years. A most convenient source is his *Decision, Order, and Time,* referred to already. The terminology and definitions of concepts are largely but not entirely those of Shackle. In the interest of continuity of argument, I will not refer to Shackle's significant work at every point at which that would be possible, but shall indicate some divergence of terminology at appropriate points.

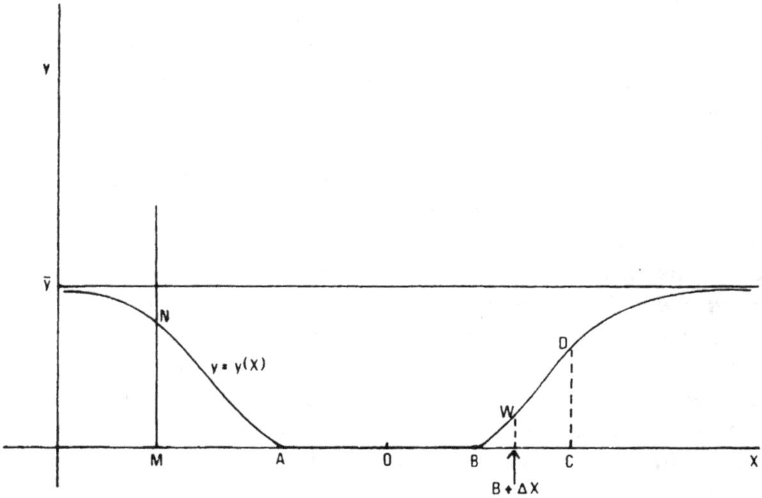

Figure 12.

represent overall gains or losses as compared with the actual capital outlay involved.

The vertical axis in the diagram measures, on the appropriate ordinal scale, the degree of potential surprise that the decision maker attaches to the various possible outcomes. To the possible outcome *OC*, for example, is attached a potential surprise of *CD*. The magnitude will have been arrived at in answer to a question as to the degree of disbelief with which the possibility of an outcome equal to *CO* was envisaged, or the degree to which, in his present state and manner of seeing things, the individual would be surprised to see the value *OC* emerge. Proceeding in similar fashion it is possible to build up the entire curve $y = y(x)$ describing the potential surprise attached to the entire range of possible outcomes.

In contemplating the possible outcomes from a decision event an individual will conceivably be able to specify a positive magnitude so large that he entertains an extremely high degree of disbelief in its possible occurrence. This may be so high that he does not regard the outcome to be possible at all. He regards it as perfectly *im*possible. A maximum degree of potential surprise is thus attached to that outcome magnitude. We have labelled that maximum potential surprise in the diagram $\bar{y}$, and drawing a horizontal line at that ordinate value have shown the potential surprise curve as asymptotic to it in the easterly direction. Similarly, the loss outcome segment of the potential surprise curve would be asymptotic to the maximum potential surprise magnitude in the westward direction.

The rates at which the respective positive and negative segments of the potential surprise curve approach the asymptote will not necessarily be the same. The one side is not necessarily the mirror image of the other. Everything depends on the determinants of the decision maker's imaginative view of things at the unique decision moment at which the various outcome possibilities are contemplated. Moreover, the potential surprise curve should perhaps in certain instances be truncated in the loss direction. Suppose, for example, that the *X* values represented wealth outcomes from an investment activity and that the magnitude *M* on the diagram represented the individual's total wealth and therefore his maximum sustainable loss. In that event the loss segment of the curve to the left of point *N*, which is vertically above the maximum sustainable loss *M*, has no meaning, so that for decision making purposes the curve should be truncated at that point.

For the present, however, we are more interested in the interpretation of the segment *AB* on the *X* variable axis. Ignoring for the present the remainder of the curve, imagine that in the decision event being contemplated the entire range of possible outcomes is described by a potential surprise curve coinciding with the *X* axis throughout its length and terminating in *A* and *B*. It can then be said that the decision maker is attaching a zero potential surprise to all possible outcomes in this range. As he sees things he would not be at all surprised if any outcome in the range *AB* occurred. For purposes of vocabulary, all outcomes in the range *AB* are conceived to be *perfectly possible* and have associated with them a *zero potential surprise.*

Continuing to imagine a function that terminates at *A* and *B*, the individual will, we suggest, *focus* his attention on only the best and the worst possible outcomes which the project offers. In reacting to the ability of this project or economic opportunity to arrest or grasp or command his attention, the individual will find his attention focused on the magnitudes *A* and *B*. These will be referred to as the *focus elements,* the focus loss and the focus gain of the project, for there is no point in an individual's being interested in the fact that an activity may bring a moderate fortune, say within the range *OB*, if it is equally possible, or in this case perfectly possible, that it will bring a considerable fortune, *OB*. At the same time there is no point in being concerned that the activity may result in moderate misfortune, say within the range *OA*, if it is likewise perfectly possible that it will result in considerable misfortune, *OA*.

"When many different things are all equally and perfectly possible," Shackle concludes, "it is the brilliant and the black extremes which hold our thoughts."[23] In the case in hand, then, we can characterize the *attention arresting power* of the project in terms of its *focus*

[23]Shackle, *Decision, Order, and Time,* p. 118. See also Shackle's *Expectation, Enterprise and Profit* (Chicago: Aldine, 1970), chapter 5.

elements A and B. In more complex and realistic cases it is perfectly conceivable that within such a range a "zero potential surprise can be assigned to each of an unlimited number of rival, mutually exclusive [outcome] hypotheses all at once; any number of suggested answers to a question . . . can all be regarded . . . as perfectly possible. The same is true of any other degree of potential surprise. . . . Potential surprise is completely nondistributional."[24]

Suppose now that a project being contemplated differs from the one we have just considered in that its range of possible outcomes extends along the X axis to the right of B and also possibly to the left of A. Its potential surprise curve can still be as shown in Figure 12, having an *inner range* of *perfectly possible* or *zero potential surprise* outcomes, but with the prospect also of other possible outcomes to which positive potential surprise is attached. Examine now the rightward segment of such a project's potential surprise curve.

A slightly higher outcome than B, say $B + \Delta X$, may be conceived to be possible, but less than perfectly possible, and it may have associated with it a positive potential surprise indicated by the point W on the curve. As the level of possible outcome is higher the degree of potential surprise will also become larger. Indeed, in view of the increasing degrees of uncertainty surrounding the higher possible outcomes, the more shadowy in the decision maker's vision the possible outcomes become, and the potential surprise associated with them will increase at an increasing rate. But for outcomes thought to be nearly impossible, the potential surprise curve will approach the magnitude $\bar{y}$ in Figure 12. It follows, then, that the rightward segment of the potential surprise curve is likely to assume the elongated S form shown in Figure 12. A comparable argument can be applied to the S form of the leftward or loss segment of the potential surprise curve also.

Now in the first of the projects we discussed, the project's *power to arrest and command the decision maker's attention* was encapsuled in the gain and loss *focus values B* and A. For the second project it may be the case that as the contemplated possible outcome increases, say to $B + \Delta X$, the attractiveness of this value, or its power to grasp or focus the decision maker's attention, will outweigh the nonzero degree of potential surprise associated with it. Thus the focus element of the project may shift from B to W. Then whereas the first project commanded attention by virtue of its focus elements A and B, the second project commands attention by virtue of *its* focus elements A and W.

[24]Shackle, *Decision, Order, and Time*, p. 70.

This nondistributional-possibility-surprise way of looking at things is summarized in the proposition that a decision maker will *focus* his attention on only two such focus elements, a focus gain and a focus loss element respectively, each represented by a point on the potential surprise curve. The corresponding outcome magnitudes are the values with power to attract or repel attention and choice.

But we can deduce a still firmer statement. Recognizing the uniqueness of the decision moment in historic time, each potential surprise curve such as *ABW* relates to a unique, nonrepeatable decision situation. The decision maker must contemplate all of the possible outcomes from the activity, extending on the *X* axis from *A* to $B + \Delta X$, and regard them *not* as possible occurrences in a series of repetitive processes, but as *rival* outcomes, only one of which can eventuate. As all of the possible outcomes are rivals and only one of them can occur, no meaning at all could be attached to any kind of averaging of them, for no repetitive processes are available to give any rationale to such an averaging process. Potential surprise is then completely nondistributional.

Opening before us now is the possibility of comparing any number or activity alternatives and making choices between them on the basis of their pairs of focus elements. For example, it becomes possible for rational choice to be made between one activity alternative presenting focus elements *A* and *B* and another presenting focus elements *A* and *W*. In relation to every line of alternative economic action it is possible to conceive of a potential surprise curve. Without cluttering Figure 12 it is possible to envisage a set of such alternatives, in relation to which a corresponding set of potential surprise curves clusters or nests in the diagram. Each such curve would have a smaller or larger inner range of zero potential surprise or perfectly possible outcomes. The gain segments of the cluster of curves will not necessarily be ordered in the eastward direction in the same sequence as the corresponding loss segments are ordered in the westward direction. But their focus elements can be specified and marshaled to lead us closer to decision criteria.

The Attractiveness Function

The decision maker, we have posited, will reduce outcome and surprise prospects to their inherent focus values. He will be attracted in a positive sense by the value magnitude of the possible outcomes, but repelled or deterred by the degrees of potential surprise associated with them. In Figure 12, for example, outcome *OC* is more attractive as to its positive magnitude than *OB*, but it is tarnished by having associated with it a potential surprise measured on the ordinal scale by CD.

To visualize the tradeoff that exists in the decision maker's mind between positive outcome and potential surprise we can construct an *activity attractiveness function*[25] and designate it as

$$R = R(x, y). \tag{1}$$

Recalling the development of the surprise function, the attractiveness function can be written in the form

$$R = R[x, y(x)]. \tag{2}$$

On the assumption that the outcome variable x can be treated as a continuous variable, the potential surprise function defined over that variable and the attractiveness function will also be continuous. Assuming continuity in the attractiveness function, a tradeoff relation between outcome magnitudes and potential surprise can be traced. But continuity is in no sense essential to the logic of the argument. It would be quite reasonable to conceive of discretely specified possible outcomes and potential surprise and still envisage their conjunction in an attractiveness function as described in Equation (2).

The following general properties of the attractiveness function can then be specified:

$$\begin{aligned} &\partial R/\partial x > 0 \text{ for } x > 0; \\ &\partial R/\partial x < 0 \text{ for } x < 0; \text{ and} \\ &\partial R/\partial y < 0 \text{ for } 0 \leq y \leq \bar{y},\ x \neq 0. \end{aligned} \tag{4}$$

Also,

$$\frac{dR}{dx} = \frac{\partial R}{\partial x} + \frac{\partial R}{\partial y} \cdot \frac{dy}{dx} = 0.$$

For a given level of attractiveness,

$$\frac{dy}{dx} = -\frac{\partial R/\partial x}{\partial R/\partial y}. \tag{5}$$

This last relation specifies the iso-attractiveness contours in the x, y plane of the basic activity attractiveness function. A possible family of such contours is shown in Figure 13.

At an outcome value of, say, x_1 on the positive side of the outcome possibilities, an ordinate at that point will cross the family of iso-

[25]Shackle refers to "the power of a hypothesis to command the decision-maker's attention" as "ascendancy." See his *Decision, Order, and Time*, p. 188, and *Expectation, Enterprise and Profit*, p. 115. In what follows, I use in place of "ascendancy" the notion of "attractiveness."

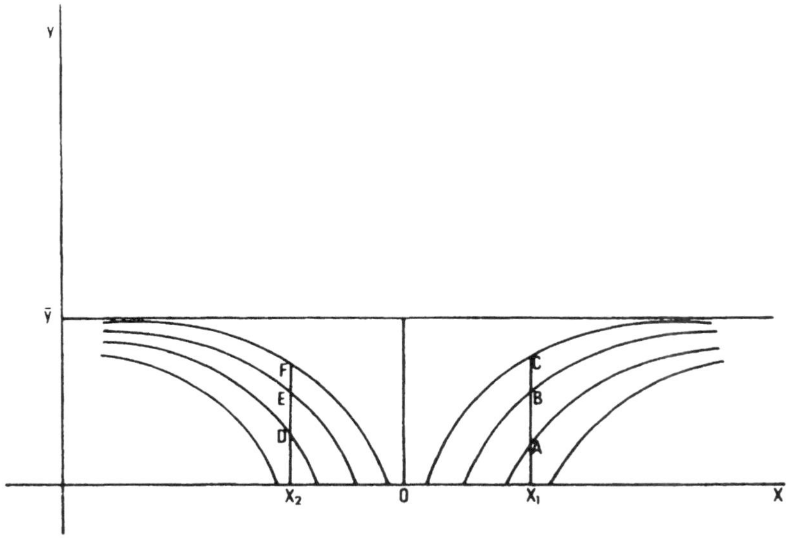

Figure 13.

attractiveness contours at points such as A, B, and C, and the increasing degrees of potential surprise designated by these points imply that the values of the attractiveness function diminish for movements in the vertical direction. Similarly, at a possible loss outcome of x_2, a vertical movement across the contours through D, E, and F will also represent a movement to progressively lower values of the attractiveness function. This is because *attractiveness* as we have defined it refers to the ability of a possible outcome to arrest or command the decision maker's attention and to focus his mind upon it. For any possible outcome, such as the gain outcome x_1 or the loss outcome x_2 in Figure 13, this "attention-commanding power" is less at C than at A in one case, and less at F than at D in the other, for in the respective cases the degrees of potential surprise with which the outcomes are contemplated are greater at C and F.

The contour lines in Figure 13 are asymptotic to, but cannot meet, the maximum potential surprise coordinate $\bar{y}$. This follows because outcomes to which $\bar{y}$ magnitudes refer are assumed to be perfectly impossible, and the decision maker cannot therefore have any logical interest in them for purposes of choice. The contour lines are indicative of the manner in which an individual reacts to changes in possible outcome values for varying degrees of potential surprise. If, then, outcomes are conceived to be impossible, no change can be envisaged and a zero attractiveness value can be assigned to every point on the $y = \bar{y}$ line.

Examining the positive segment of possible outcome values, a rightward movement across the family of contours will bring us to higher values of the activity attractiveness function. Putting these ideas together, the decision maker will find his interest focused on a combination of possible outcome and potential surprise. This will apply in both the gain and the loss segments of the analysis. The manner in which the focus values are identified and influence decisions can now be indicated quite readily. But in anticipation of this it will be helpful to consider a possible difficulty that might be raised in connection with the argument.

Utility and Probability Reappraised

Utility

It could be an understandable inference to interpret the attractiveness function as an implicit utility function defined over outcome and potential surprise, and to see the contour lines as indifference curves in the traditional sense. Obviously there is a *formal* similarity between the neoclassical utility function and our attractiveness function, but the differences provide good grounds for keeping the vocabulary quite distinct.

The utility function, or the expected utility function considered in Part II above, was defined over the moments, principally the mean and the variance, of the subjectively assigned probability distribution of a random variable. But in the potential surprise analysis of this chapter, the probability underpinning has been abandoned completely in favor of a nondistributional variable approach. There is therefore no warrant for speaking of expectations and associated dispersions in a mathematical-statistical sense, and such a procedure has been deprived of legitimacy. Any tradeoff that arises in this new way of looking at things necessarily has a different connotation and is embedded in a very different specification of variables.

After all that has been said about the uniqueness of the decision situation in historic time and the logical inability to recapture it and decide again after it has gone, the activity attractiveness function is also *tied uniquely to a specified decision moment.* At each point in time at which a decision is made, a new attractiveness function must be created, dislodging the old as events and attitudes are reshaped. Any notion of an intertemporally stable utility function comports best with the static, not with the dynamic evolution that belongs to the world of fact. Utility analysis and its associated vocabulary has meaningful reference only to the timeless and static constructs of neoclassical theory.

Probability

It may be imagined also that the potential surprise curve can in fact be regarded as essentially a probability distribution turned upside down, and that all that has been said about potential surprise can be transformed into statements about probability. The suggestion may be encountered that the potential surprise attached to a possible outcome can be interpreted as unity minus the probability of its occurrence. But this would evince a failure to understand fully the decision apparatus which is here being proposed, and it would overlook some important and fundamental distinctions.[26]

What Shackle's basic theory proposes is the notion of *potential* surprise, and this requires us to bear in mind all that has been said regarding the *uniqueness* of the decision event and the decision maker's stance at a unique point in the flow of historic time. *Potential* surprise refers to an individual's assessment of what he feels *now*, at the decision point, would be the surprise he would feel in the future if a possible outcome were to occur. There is no logical meaning, as we have already argued in Chapter 2, in the comparison between *surprise actually experienced* at one point in time and the *potential surprise* with which a possible outcome was contemplated at an anterior point in time. Each such temporal point has its own uniqueness. But more particularly, the transformation of potential surprise, based on degrees of disbelief, into probability, which is grounded on the contrary in degrees of belief, is prohibited in large numbers of economic-financial decisions by the fact that the occurrence of decisions at temporally separate and discrete dates makes it logically impossible to regard the decision events as repetitive or replicatable.

Consider now the fact that our argument anchored the potential surprise curve in the reality of *perfect possibility*. It would be well beyond our province to inquire into the psychological foundations that prepare an individual to take observable and describable attitudes to situations and possibilities and events. All that we have posited is that as the individual surveys the range of possible outcomes he *is* able to say that there is a range of outcomes, a subset of the entire possibilities, such that he would *not be at all surprised* if any one of them were to occur. Such an *inner range* need not be large. It may be quite small. The important thing is that, small or large, this is a range of outcomes that the decision maker regards as *perfectly possible* and to which, therefore, he attaches *zero potential surprise*.

[26]On this important point, see again the lengthy discussions in Shackle *Decision, Order, and Time*, especially Part II, including chapters 11 and 12 on "Critics of Potential Surprise" and "A Counter-critique on Probability." Cf. the discussion in Nicholas Georgescu-Roegen, *Analytical Economics* (Cambridge: Harvard Univ. Press, 1966), pp. 260ff. and chapter 6 passim on "The Nature of Expectation and Uncertainty."

To make probability transformations out of this would involve a gigantic leap. For what *probability* is to be taken as representing perfect *possibility*? Is it unity? But the analysis speaks of perfect *possibility* and *not* perfect *certainty,* for the whole tenor and motivation of the ideas is *un*certainty. Moreover, there is nothing to prevent our saying that any number of outcomes are perfectly possible, and therefore assigning to them all a zero potential surprise.

What is more, it is quite reasonable to assign perfect possibility to both a possible outcome and its contradictory. Irrevocably this is involved when we invoke the *uniqueness* of the decision event, for from a given decision only one actual outcome can eventuate. What, then, would be the probability it might be wished to associate with our uncertanity concept of perfect possibility? In the light of what has been said it cannot be unity. But then on what grounds is it possible to say that *any* designatable probability magnitude corresponds to perfect possibility? "Should we not rather say that there is *no* natural and self-justifying basis for a mapping of probability on possibility, and therefore, on potential surprise?"[27]

This does not deny that the decision maker's judgments as to possibility and potential surprise may arise in part out of objectively given frequency ratios described in historically generated data. Yet regardless of information, fashions, and even the conventional reliance on the likelihood that the outcomes of tomorrow will be like the events of yesterday, it does *not* follow that potential surprise can be *mapped into* probability. A hypothesis may, from a probability point of view, be rendered more improbable merely by a change in an individual's knowledge as time passes and introduces additional hypotheses, even though the first hypothesis is *in itself* quite unaffected by such new knowledge. Against all such changes as these, however, potential surprise is invariant.

If, moreover, a probability distribution of outcomes is assigned *before* a decision to a variable that can assume only a single outcome value, the emergent result will imply that in some sense a faulty judgment was made. This need not be so with potential surprise, for "the use of a nondistributional variable enables the net of nonsurprising hypotheses to be spread as wide as the individual thinks needful."[28] In connection with repetitive experiments the idea of a probability distribution can find a haven. In such a case the foundation postulate that Mossin invoked, the postulate that financial theory deals with "choices among probability distributions," would have

[27]Shackle, Ibid., p. 71.
[28]Ibid., p. 77.

meaning.[29] But this, we have argued, is simply not the case in large numbers of economic-financial decisions.

Financial-economic choices involve preponderantly unique decisions under uncertainty, and the "unsureness" that abounds can not invoke the probability methods that sweep uncertainty away.[30]

Decision Criteria

We assume now that an individual confronting a unique decision situation is considering the advisibility of adopting an activity for which he has described a potential surprise curve such as is shown in Figure 12, and that there exist also the iso-attractiveness contours from an attractiveness function as described in Figure 13. These ideas are now brought together in Figure 14.

In stressing the focus gain and loss outcomes, Shackle has suggested a method of deriving the decision criterion implicit in the analysis. In Figure 12 the point *W* on the potential surprise curve may be such a focus value. In Figure 14 the rightward or the gain segment of the potential surprise curve will, after it leaves its inner range along the *X*

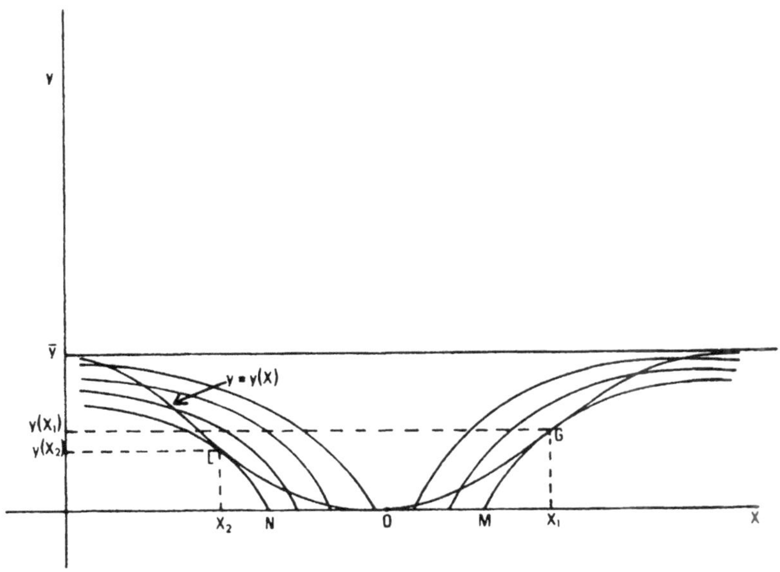

Figure 14.

[29]Mossin, *Theory of Financial Markets*, p. 6.

[30]Cf. Shackle, *Decision, Order, and Time*, chapter 10, "Potential Surprise Axiomatized," for further discussion.

axis, rise at first across increasingly higher valued iso-attractiveness contours until it reaches the highest attainable contour at point G. As the curve continues to rise beyond that point it will traverse progressively lower-valued contours. At point G the potential surprise curve is tangential to an iso-attractiveness contour.

Now the point G, or its coordinates, $[x_1, y(x_1)]$, describes the *primary focus gain* of the activity under consideration. The power of this activity to command or focus the decision maker's attention is concentrated in that point. Similarly, point L, or its coordinates, $[x_2, y(x_2)]$, describes the *primary focus loss* of the activity.[31] As the decision maker contemplates the pulling power of the choice open to him the pair of focus elements G and L will loom uppermost as ultimate prospects.

But a method that will enable the individual to *discriminate between* alternatives is required as a decision criterion. In Figure 14 consider the iso-attractiveness contour passing through G. Clearly, point M on the outcome axis is the zero potential surprise equivalent of G, lying as it does on the same contour, and it provides the same degree of attractiveness as the primary focus gain of the activity in question. In Shackle's terminology, M is the *standardized focus gain.*[32] By similar reasoning, N is the *standardized focus loss*. It is then *this* pair of values, the *standardized focus outcomes*, which will determine the appeal of the activity to the decision maker's imagination. For every activity alternative a pair of standardized focus outcomes can be extracted and these become decisive as a discriminating decision criterion.

The relation between the standardized focus outcomes can now be embodied on a *decision map*, as shown in Figure 15.[33] Point A is described by coordinates M and N, the standardized focus gain and loss generated by the activity whose characteristics were considered in Figure 14. There may exist simultaneously another activity alternative which generates point D on the same decision map. Activity D yields both a lower standardized focus gain and a lower standardized focus loss. If, however, the decision maker so interpreted his own personal situation, preferences, and predilections as to deem projects A and D equally attractive, they would lie on the same indifference curve. The decision map, or the standardized focus gain-loss space, will contain indifference curves that partition the space interior to, but not necessarily including, the maximum loss boundary.

[31]Again the terminology is due to Shackle, *Decision, Order, and Time*.

[32]Ibid., pp. 161ff.

[33]Shackle has introduced this concept under the designation of the "gambler indifference map" in his *Decision, Order, and Time*, p. 162, and as the "investment indifference map" in *Expectation, Enterprise and Profit*, p. 122.

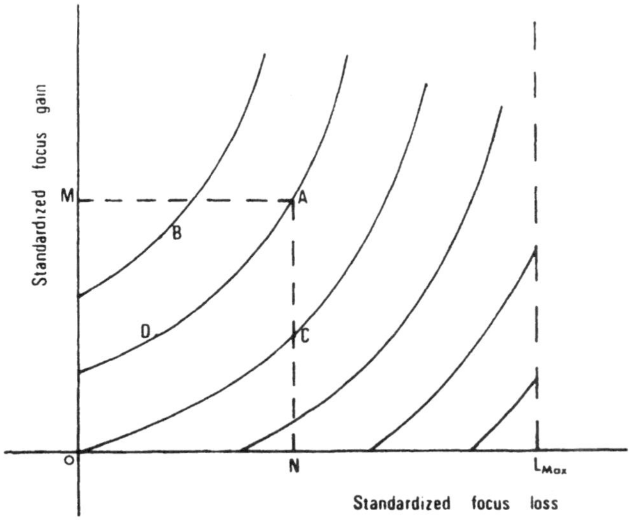

Figure 15.

On the loss axis of the diagram the vertical intercept L_{max} indicates the maximum loss which the decision maker can sustain. Decision indifference curves may in some instances abut this effective boundary. Or they may assume steeply positive slopes that make them asymptotic to, or perhaps quite distanced from, such a boundary. But the slope of the indifference curve in the decision map space reflects the rate at which the decision maker is prepared to trade off standardized gain and loss in his overall evaluation of projects. In general, steeper indifference curves record greater degrees of uncertainty-aversion. For in that case a larger increment in standardized focus gain is required to offset an increment of standardized focus loss.

A number of other properties of the decision map can be explored. First, an indifference curve will conceivably emanate from the origin of the map. In Shackle's terminology this can be referred to as the *origin indifference curve,* and it will describe the locus of projects which are equivalent to inaction or to holding investable resources in cash with the prospect of neither gain nor loss.[34] Consider on the origin indifference curve the project C, which is vertically below A and offers the prospect of the same standardized focus loss, N, as does project A. We say then that project A *dominates* project C, for it offers the prospect of a larger standardized focus gain together with the same size standardized focus loss.

[34]Shackle, *Nature of Economic Thought,* p. 175.

The project decision criterion, then, inheres in the rule that it will be economically worthwhile if its standardized gain-loss coordinates place it to the northwest of the origin indifference curve. For the choice *between* projects, or for the *ranking* in order of desirability, the rule follows that that project is most preferred which lies on the highest attainable indifference curve removed in the northwest direction from the origin indifference curve. In Figure 15, project *B*, offering both a lower standardized focus gain and a lower standardized focus loss than project *A*, is nevertheless the preferred or dominating project.

These ideas, then, fulfill the promise of a theory of decision making in conditions of true uncertainty. Remaining now is the task of applying it to financial market and other economic decisions, thereby escaping from the strictures imposed in conventional theory by the continual assumption of equilibrium postures.

9

Applications to Investment Decisions

In this concluding chapter I bring together the threads of my analysis and consider its application to investment decisions in the corporate firm and to financial investment or the choice of financial asset portfolios. In each case, I shall keep in perspective the decision maker's need to consider his best next move from the inherited situation in which his act of choice is located. His inheritance, and the act of choice following from it, are always uniquely located in the flow of historic time. Attention will accordingly be focused on *marginal* criteria for action and on the worthwhileness of incremental variations of policies and economic behavior.

In the financial asset market at any point in time the principal data observable are the prices of the assets traded, corporate common stocks, debt capital and other senior securities, and the securities of government and personal borrowers. Implicit in those prices are the effective yields or prospective rates of return that can be earned by holding the assets. This effective yield is an input to the determination of the cost of capital from the borrower's point of view.[1] It will be assumed for present purposes that the mathematical properties of these relationships are well understood, and I shall concentrate in what follows on the incorporation of such relations into our required investment decision criteria.[2]

[1]The determination of this asset yield has been discussed widely in the financial literature and in the theory of capital. A unique solution value of it may not exist if some of the elements of the cash flows stream promised by the asset are negative. For an early discussion of this "multiple root" problem, see J. H. Lorie and L. J. Savage, "Three Problems in Rationing Capital," *Journal of Business* (October 1955), reprinted in Ezra Solomon, ed., *The Management of Corporate Capital* (Chicago: Free Press of Glencoe for the Graduate School of Business, Univ. of Chicago, 1959).

[2]Cf. the several relevant papers in the Ezra Solomon volume referred to in footnote 1 above, and also in Archer and D'Ambrosio, *Theory of Business Finance;* Bierman and Hass, *Introduction to Management Finance;* Haley and Schall, *Theory of Financial Decisions;* and Vickers, *Theory of the Firm*, chapter 1.

Investment in the Firm

Assume for the present that the decision maker in a firm is able to specify (1) the periodic cash inflow, S_t, which will be generated in each future period by a specified investment project; (2) the discount factor, or the "cost of capital," m, at which the future expected cash flows should be discounted to determine their present economic value; and (3) the time horizon over which such a valuation should be made, or the number of time periods in the economic life of the asset. In such a case the basic valuation relation can be stated as

$$V_0 = \sum_{t=1}^{n} S_t/(1 + m)^t. \tag{1}$$

with V_0 describing the economic value.

The discount factor, m, has been referred to as a measure of the firm's cost of capital, and our motivation for this lies in our earlier discussion of that variable. The cost of capital is taken to be the minimum required rate of return that must be earned on investing marginal money capital in the firm in order to avoid a dilution of the shareholders' wealth position. In this sense the cost of capital is interpretable as a true economic opportunity cost. This capital cost datum was referred to previously as the full marginal cost of relaxing the firm's money capital availability constraint.

Taking this cost of capital, the economic value of the activity can be determined by discounting the cash flow expectations at a discount factor equal to it. If it is supposed that the entire money capital outlay is made at the time of the investment decision, the decision criterion can be put in the form

$$V_0 \gtreqless C_0 \tag{2}$$

where C_0 refers to the necessary capital outlay. Not all of the necessary capital expenditure may be made in the same time period as that of the decision moment, so that a somewhat more general statement of the decision criterion will be

$$\sum_{t=1}^{n} S_t/(1 + m)^t \gtreqless \sum_{t=1}^{n} C_t/(1 + m)^t, \tag{3}$$

with the recognition that not all the elements of the S_t stream may be positive.

The Standardized Focus Decision Criterion

The following relies on the analytical foundations and diagrams of Chapter 8. For the present application it will be assumed that a *potential surprise curve* can be described for the cash flow associated with the proposed activity *in each time period* of its economic life. Given the range over which the periodic cash flows are defined, the decision maker can also specify a family of iso-attractiveness contours, and the juxtaposition of the potential surprise curve and the iso-attractiveness contours *for each time period* will provide a focus gain element and a focus loss element for each period. From these the *standardized focus gain and loss elements* follow, and they can be transposed, in ways we shall now examine, to a decision map in the standardized focus element space.

Consider now the potential surprise curve referable to the cash flow of tth time period for the jth project. Taking the X axis of the diagram in Figure 12 of Chapter 8 as measuring the money values of the tth period's cash flow, positive and negative values can be marked off to the right and left of zero respectively. A negative cash flow could result either because capital expenditure was made in that period, or because the revenue generated by the activity fell below its operating costs.

Proceeding as before it will be possible to determine the *standardized focus gain* and the *standardized focus loss* of this tth period's cash flow for the jth project. This being given, the implied streams of standardized focus elements can be reduced to their present discounted values at a discount factor equal to the opportunity cost of money capital.

Employing the symbols G_{SF} and L_{SF} to denote these present discounted values, and using M_t and N_t as the tth period's standardized focus gain and loss elements, we have

$$G_{SF} = \sum_{t=1}^{n} M_t/(1 + m)^t \tag{4}$$

and similarly,

$$L_{SF} = \sum_{t=1}^{n} N_t/(1 + m)^t. \tag{5}$$

The G_{SF} and L_{SF}, that is, the jth project's overall gain (standardized focus) and loss (standardized focus), may then be brought into relation with each other on a familiar decision map.

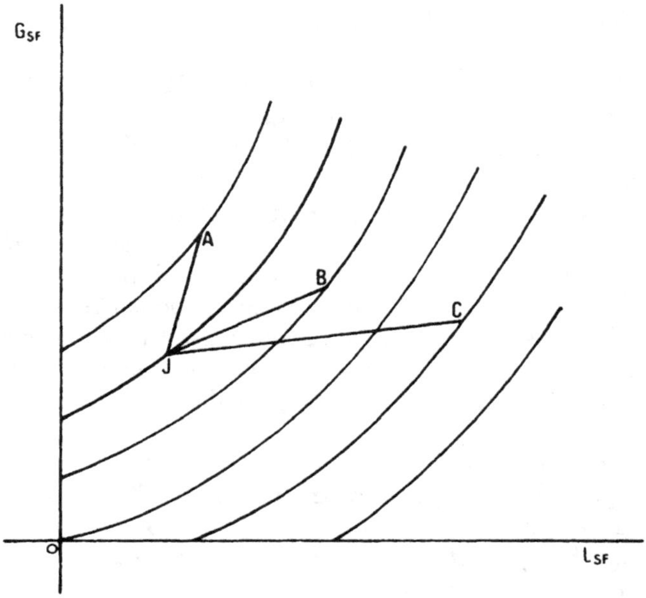

Figure 16.

This is shown in Figure 16 as the point *J* in the $G_{SF} - L_{SF}$ space. In the situation envisaged the economic viability of the project is established by reason that the point *J* lies on an indifference locus to the northwest of the origin indifference curve. It follows that other activity alternatives, say projects *i* and *k*, not shown on the decision map, could be compared with project *J*, assuming a comparable capital outlay and a similar economic life were involved. If different capital outlays and different economic lives were involved in comparisons between projects, combinations of opportunities and considerations of reinvestments of capital for specifiable time periods would have to be brought into the analysis in order to achieve strict economic comparability.

A question that arises in connection with the decision map relates to the manner in which the desirability of possible investment activities may be affected by a variation in the rate of interest, or in the yields available on financial assets. We are concerned here with the impact on a firm's capital expenditure of a change (a reduction, say) in its cost of capital or in the full marginal cost of relaxing its money capital availability constraint. It follows from the arithmetic of the case that at a lower discount rate the present value of a given cash flow stream of a given duration will be higher. It may appear, then, that as the interest rate and therefore the cost of capital falls, investment projects will become more attractive and investment expenditures will increase. If this were so we could envisage a more or less smooth southeast-sloping investment function of the familiar neoclassical form. But the answer is not as simple as that, and we must be somewhat agnostic as to the outcome following a reduction in the cost of capital.

The outcome turns on the time shapes of the cash flow streams, or the magnitudes in different time periods of the standardized focus gain and loss elements referable to the project. Consider the M_t and N_t vectors in Equations (4) and (5). If there is a reduction in m, then there will occur an increase in *both* the G_{SF} and L_{SF}, with implications for the possible change in the location of the project J decision point in Figure 16. Given the simultaneous increases in *both* the L_{SF} and the G_{SF}, the overall effect could move the decision point from J to one of the points A, B, or C. A move to A would imply that the increase in the gain value more than offsets the increase in the loss value, as A stands on an indifference locus to the northwest of that passing through J. In such a case the reduction in the cost of capital has increased the attractiveness of the investment opportunity, and the relationship between investment expenditure and the cost of capital is of the normal neoclassical kind.

It could well be the case, however, that the reduction in m could shift the project decision point from J to B. At this latter point the project is less attractive than before, with B dominated by J. This is the case in which the relation between investment and the cost of capital runs counter to that generally posited in neoclassical theory. This uncovers what has become an intense ground of debate in recent years under the name of "reswitching" and "capital reversal" in the theory of capital. Conceptually, with judgment reserved on empirical significance, a lower cost of capital may actually diminish capital investment expenditures.[3]

In Figure 16 the movement of the project's decision point from J to B still leaves the project economically worthwhile, for B is on an indifference curve to the northwest of the origin indifference curve. If, however, the induced change in the relation between G_{SF} and L_{SF} had moved the decision point from J to C, then the project would have fallen below the minimum level of economic worthwhileness, as C lies to the southeast of the origin indifference curve.

[3]Cf. Shackle, *Decision, Order, and Time*, pp. 238, 290, and for an extensive examination of the controversy on the capital reversal problem see Harcourt, *Some Cambridge Controversies*. The analysis in this chapter of both investment in the firm and asset portfolio choice is again heavily indebted to Shackle.

Financial Asset Returns

The remaining task is to exhibit the implications of the analysis for the investor's choice of his financial asset portfolio and for changes in it at any given time. The relevant criteria revolve again about the standardized focus gains and losses referable to the holding of specific assets. But whereas in the real investment project decision the standardized focus gain and loss values were summed over a number of specified time periods, in the present case the summation will be *across* specified assets at a *given* time period.

Out dissent from the timeless, static portfolio theory forces us to be primarily concerned again with the best next moves that individual investors might make at definable points in time. Our argument will not be directed to questions of generalized equilibrium relationships. Because time passes and does not stand still; because inheritances, perceptions, knowledge, and conventions change; our analysis must refuse to lock decision processes into artificial constructs built on assumptions that envisage precisely the contrary.

Moreover, not only do we thus avoid an analytical capitulation to the timelessness and the stationary nature of the theory we exhibited and evaluated in Part II, but we recognize also that the question before the financial investor is *not* that of selecting an optimum asset portfolio *in the sense envisaged by* that theory. For if the assumptions in which the theory itself is grounded do demonstrable violence to the realities of the world, its validity or empirical viability is of necessity suspect. We make this statement in full recognition, of course, of the positivist prescriptions insisting that "the test of a theory is the success of its predictions."[4] But we are entitled to question whether positivist prediction that leaves the decision maker in virtual agnosticism as to the true *causation* and *explanation* involved in his position can be properly sustained.

The argument that follows does not call for *less* empirical data or investigations of the relationships that have emerged in the past and on which the formation of conventions may depend. Against all such data and information available the investor at a point in time makes his best estimates of the rates of return that various assets may provide during a defined period of time, which we shall refer to as his *decision horizon*. The decision horizon is a defined length of calendar time as it is perceived by an individual *at an actual moment of decision*.

In this it is *not* being said that the investor will make no further changes in his asset choice during the lapse of time between his decision moment and the terminus of his decision horizon. We shall admit,

[4]Cf. Hollis and Nell, *Rational Economic Man*, p. 10.

in other words, of the possibility that *trading* in assets acquired or held at the decision moment may occur during the interval within the decision horizon.

This implies that the decision horizon as initially specified is to be understood as a real time span as seen by the decision maker *at the time of decision*, and that if trading occurs during that interval the decision horizon has by that fact been terminated and a *new* decision moment with its *own* decision horizon has been specified. The specification *at each decision moment* of a corresponding decision horizon is a way of tentatively tying down time in order to estimate what might be the rates of return earned on the holding of various assets during that period.

The decision horizon is not to be understood, therefore, as the same as, and it does not define, the *holding period* over which assets will be held. The decision to effect a trade in a financial asset implies that a change in portfolio composition is being effected at that date and a tradeoff is made between one financial asset and another. At the moment of trading, a new evaluation of portfolio opportunities and prospects is made, the evaluations made at the previous decision moment are no longer necessarily relevant, and a new formulation of the decision criteria must at that moment be confronted.

In the conventional theory of asset selection, which lies at the foundation of the equilibrium theory of financial asset prices, it is assumed that the period over which an asset or a portfolio position would be held was specified *ab initio,* and that all transactors in the financial asset market actually defined the same asset holding period. In the approach we are adopting here, however, the asset holding period is variable. Turning aside from the strictures of the equilibrium theory that ignores market trading activity, we take account of the impact on portfolio choice and behavior of the possibility that trading may occur. To the extent that trading does occur, capital gains or losses may be realized, and such *actual* gains or losses will conceivably make the *realized* returns on assets quite different from the expected value of a probability distribution of a specified holding period return. The possibility of false trading again enters, with implications for changes in wealth positions and effective market endowments.

By financial asset returns, then, we mean the *expectation* that the decision maker holds *at his decision moment* regarding the various possible levels of the rate of return that might be realized on an asset during his horizon period, *taking account of the possibility* that the market value of the asset *may* rise to a pre-specified critical level during that period, and that if it does, his corresponding portfolio position will be liquidated and the capital gain will be taken. This being given, we can then suppose the investor to hold in his mind at his decision moment a potential surprise function defined as before over the range of possible rates of return as thus conceived.

Potential Surprise in Rates of Return

In discussing the decision map, I interpreted Shackle's origin indifference curve as a locus of decision points that would be equivalent in an individual's mind to his doing nothing with his investable resources and holding them in non–income-earning cash. Now a realistic investment option is that of placing funds in a "risk-free" asset, say government securities that are risk-free as to their income stream but which are subject to uncertain changes in capital values as interest rates fluctuate. For purposes of the analysis, I refer to the rate of return available on such an asset as a "risk-free" yield, designated as R_F.

The potential surprise curves described in Figure 17 relate to two different assets *A* and *B* respectively. Each curve is assumed to have an inner range of "perfectly possible" or "zero potential surprise" rates of return, and to describe different degrees of disbelief in the occurrence of higher and lower possible rates of return outside of this range. Some new aspects arise, however, in the application of the potential surprise curve to portfolio asset choice.

The horizontal axis measures the possible rates of return, *R*, which may be realized on an asset in the sense we indicated in the preceding

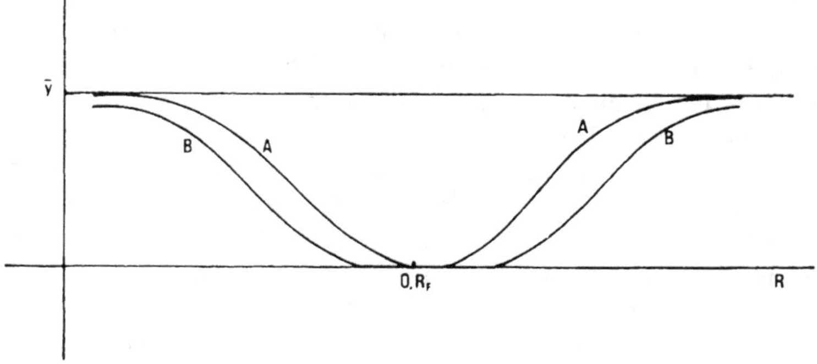

Figure 17.

section. But within the inner range a zero point is labeled both zero and R_F, to indicate that the horizontal axis may be marked off in two different scales. If actual rates of return were measured on this axis the rates could be understood to be spread on either side of the risk-free rate R_F. But if R_F is taken as the zero point, then the positive and negative values to the right and the left measure the possible divergence of rates of return from the available alternative R_F rate. We shall work in what follows with variations from the zero point in order to achieve a close analogy with our previous concepts of focus gains and losses, and negative rates of return will signify deviations below the risk-free rate of interest.

As previously, we marry the potential surprise curves to a portfolio manager's family of iso-attractiveness contours and thereby determine both the primary focus gain and loss rates of return and the corresponding standardized focus gain and loss elements. In Figure 18 the primary focus gain and loss elements for asset A are shown as R_{A1} and R_{A2} respectively, and those for asset B as R_{B1} and R_{B2}. The corresponding standardized focus elements can be read off the positive and negative rate of return scale, normalized around R_F as the zero point, as M_A, N_A and M_B, N_B respectively.

In the decision map shown in Figure 19 the origin indifference curve is now to be understood as emanating from the risk-free rate R_F, and the decision maker would reject asset opportunities in the subspace to the southeast of this curve. The axes of the diagram measure

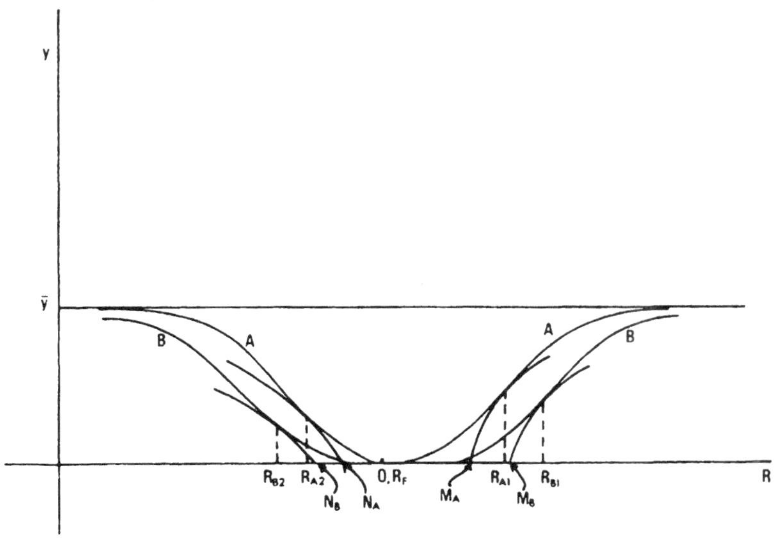

Figure 18.

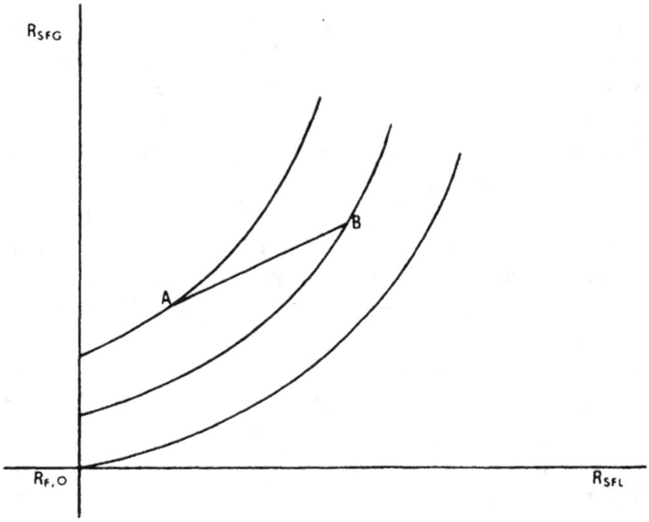

Figure 19.

in the vertical direction the standardized focus gain rate of return, R_{SFG}, and in the horizontal direction the standardized focus loss rate of return, R_{SFL}. The points *A* and *B* on the diagram transcribe the M_A, N_A and the M_B, N_B values from Figure 18. In this hypothetical example, asset *A* has both a lower standardized focus gain and a lower standardized focus loss than asset *B*. Yet *A* lies on a higher indifference curve than *B*, and it would therefore be the preferred asset choice.

Before this last conclusion is reached unreservedly, however, the possible advantages of diversification must be probed. Rates of return generated by asset *A* may be independent of those realized from holding asset *B*. Alternatively, the economic nature of assets *A* and *B* may be such that their fortunes could well fluctuate in opposite directions, so that the advantages of diversification may follow from a portfolio combination of the two assets. In that case an investor may achieve a standardized focus gain and loss combination on the linear locus *AB* by investing in a weighted combination of the assets. The resulting *portfolio standardized focus gain rate of return* is denoted by M_P and the corresponding *portfolio standardized focus loss rate of return* by N_P in the following relations. The respective portfolio weights of assets *A* and *B* will be designated by W_A and W_B, subject to $W_A + W_B = 1$. The following definitions will form the basis of more complex cases in the ensuing discussion.

$$M_P = W_A M_A + W_B M_B; \tag{6}$$

$$N_P = W_A N_A + W_B N_B. \tag{7}$$

The W_A magnitude in Equation (7) is the same as that in Equation (6), the same applying also to W_B.

Diversification, of course, is important, and far from denying its significance, our analysis must bring it clearly into view. But let us proceed cautiously. For it is in no sense true that financial asset investors are necessarily interested in diversification or that they avail themselves of the apparent advantages of it. In the first place, our theory has been designed to accommodate also the asset choices of speculative investors whose main interest may be in the returns that follow from ferreting out securities that promise appreciation in market value during their decision horizon. Such individuals may be interested in diversification to only a minimal extent, if at all.

Certain investors, moreover, avoid diversification and concentrate their investments in assets, say common stock securities, of a particular kind. Specialized mutual funds hold asset portfolios designed in this way. Likewise, appropriate information on asset investment alternatives is not inexpensive for all investors of all portfolio sizes, and transactions costs may inhibit diversification for small investors.

The notion of diversification, moreover, may be in danger of acquiring a mystique, which is not reflected in actual market activity, from the influence of the logical results of the equilibrium theory of financial asset prices. It was seen previously that in full generalized equilibrium all investors would, under the assumptions of that theory, hold the same portfolio of risky assets. It is known, of course, that in no instance is diversification actually carried to those limits.

But apart from these cautions about the extent of diversification in fact, an investor may choose to construct a portfolio combining assets A and B in such a way that he settles on the locus AB in Figure 19. The following points in relation to that kind of portfolio decision therefore require elaboration.

Portfolio Choice

Generalizing from the arguments underlying Equations (6) and (7), portfolio standardized focus gain and loss rates of return may be defined as

$$M_p = \sum_i w_i M_i \tag{8}$$

and

$$N_p = \sum_i w_i N_i. \tag{9}$$

In Figure 20 the resulting portfolio posture is described by the point P. We may ignore for the moment the arrowheads emanating from this point.

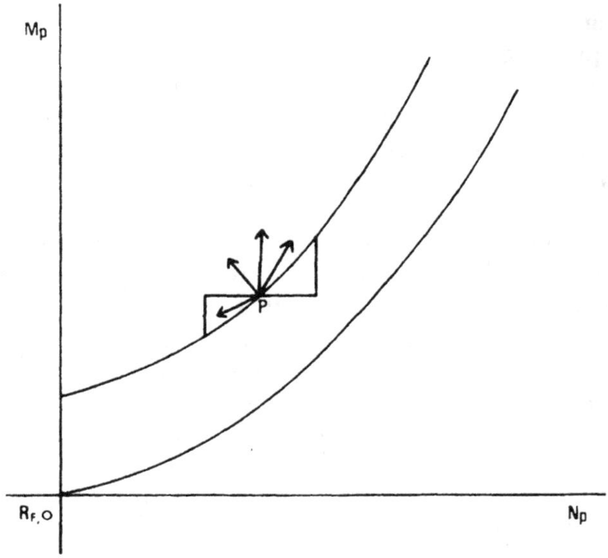

Figure 20.

It is possible, of course, that in the outcome the actual rate of return realized on the portfolio would not be as high as the ordinate intercept from the point P, or as low as the abscissa intercept. The M_i and the N_i in the summations in Equations (8) and (9) are the standardized *focus* elements of the assets in question. And actual outcomes may well diverge from those on which, in the now familiar manner, attention was focused for decision making purposes. It is, in fact, the divergences of outcomes from earlier decision foci which may give rise to changes in investment policy.

Recalling the earlier development it can now be acknowledged that investment in, say, corporate common stocks partakes forcibly of the same elements of uniqueness as do other decision situations. It may be thought, on the contrary, that the generation of an annual rate of return on the common stock of, say, the jth firm from among the population of firms listed on the New York Stock Exchange could be regarded as a genuinely random process. In such a case it may be suggested that the return on the stock could be describable by a probability distribution reflecting historically realized rates of return, or, perhaps, by a subjectively assigned probability distribution. But unfortunately, too easy a reliance on this interpretation betrays a failure to apprehend the meaning of historic economic time, its uniqueness and unidirectional movement, with all of its implications we have explored.

In a highly significant sense today's decision to invest in the *j*th firm's common stock is in fact a unique decision. It is unique because the *j*th firm today is not the same firm as the *j*th firm yesterday, or two or five years or a decade ago. Hence the annual rate of return on the *j*th firm's common stock can not be regarded as the outcome of a random process, and the familiar probability calculus cannot be applied to the description of it. Moreover, a further element of uniqueness arises from the possible realization of available capital gains during a decision horizon, as distinct from the comparison of capital values at the beginning and end of a year or a predetermined holding period. It follows that the rates of return available on various assets should properly be treated as nondistributional variables for incorporation into a theory of decisions under uncertainty as exhibited in Figures 18 and 19 above.

Nevertheless some purchasers of financial assets do diversify to a greater or lesser extent, and the investor's choice of the portfolio represented by *P* in Figure 20 may be the result of a policy choice analogous with a decision to choose a vector combination somewhere on the locus *AB* in Figure 19. But our inability to regard the asset rate of return as a distributional variable—firms change their technologies, factor intensities, operating structures, financing mix, market penetrations, product outputs, activity diversifications, and expansion policies—has other implications.

Precluded thereby is a reliance, in a definitive decision theoretic sense, on an extrapolation of a statistically quantified distribution of an asset's returns, or of a supposedly specified variance-covariance matrix of a set of asset returns. Second, the fact that we are dealing with nondistributional variables means that there are not available to us any distributional parameters, such as the moments of probability distributions, for incorporation into any kind of decision objective function. It is not possible to speak meaningfully of an expected utility function defined over the moments, for example the mean and the variance, of a probability distribution of a portfolio rate of return, for the foundations that might provide the logical justificaiton for such a procedure do not exist.

Investor diversification, then, must be based on a broader range of considerations, many of them involving qualitative rather than quantitative variables, and not on a severely, mechanistically quantified set of posited statistical relationships. But saying this adds richness to the decision process itself, and it recognizes the true nature of judgment in the economic world for what it really is. This judgment, which Haley and Schall have referred to in a different context as "the informed judgment of management," is no doubt embedded in deeper layers of psychological and sociocultural motivation, preference patterns, and predilections than we need to examine at this point.[5]

But the judgment involved at the various levels of decisions needs to be "informed," that is, economically informed judgment. And it is here that the discipline of economic history and statistical description becomes inexorably important. Suppose we make heroic assumptions regarding the continued identity of business firms and estimate their historically generated "beta coefficients," that is, the historic regression of their common stock rates of return on the similarly measured rate of return on all Stock Exchange common stocks combined. Depending on the extent to which investors *do* assume the convention that such statistical data are a meaningful guide to the future, reliance *may* be placed on the data as *pointers* to the *kinds* of relationships that might exist in the future, and which might be taken now as inputs in present decision situations.

But that, we should insist, is the precise epistemological potential of such statistical data as is, and which in the interest of maximum information must be, generated or collected. It in no sense provides a warrant for regarding as distributional variables what adequate logical and empirical considerations join in insisting are nondistributional variables. And our decision-theoretic methodology must be determined accordingly.

Judgment, which connotes responsible choice deliberation, therefore leads to a specification of an investor's financial asset portfolio in terms of M_P and N_P in Equations (8) and (9). By summation over the portfolio assets, as in these equations, we have conceived of the portfolio standardized focus gain and loss rates of return, as at P in Figure 20. The selection of P will have involved judgmental and qualitative inputs inducing larger or smaller degrees of asset portfolio diversification, or the qualitative, judgmental determination of the w_i asset weights in the equations.

We turn now to the set of factors that enter the decision nexus at any time to determine the best next move that a decision maker should adopt in the situation he has inherited. This involves the theory of portfolio change, which is already implicit in the theory of asset selection.

Portfolio Change

Consider the point P in Figure 20 and recall the estimation of its standardized focus gain and loss coordinates as $M_P = \Sigma_i w_i M_i$ and $N_P = \Sigma_i w_i N_i$ respectively. We conceive now of a portfolio trade, the pur-

[5]Haley and Schall, *Theory of Financial Decisions*, p. 249.

chase or sale of an asset or of part of an asset holding, perhaps in favor of securities previously excluded from the portfolio.

The judgments that the investor must make at the decision moment call for the estimation, in the same manner as previously, of the portfolio standardized focus gain and loss rates of return as it is estimated they will appear after the proposed portfolio change has been affected. In the arrowheads in Figure 20, we have indicated the possible directions in which the M_P, N_P portfolio coordinates may move as a result of the contemplated change, on the premise that the change will be effected only if it promises to move the decision maker to the northwest of the initial portfolio point P.

Consistent with the methodology to this point, this criterion establishes the ***primary desideratum*** of a proposed portfolio change, and it is in this sense that we shall investigate its properties in what follows. But at the same time, it is realized that what we shall see as the *prima facie* good and the *prima facie* bad may be subject to modification at the margin of decision if considerations of diversification again enter the picture.

Let us enumerate the possible benchmark criteria for the economic worthwhileness of the portfolio change. First, visualizing the new portfolio asset combination and the tentative judgment as to portfolio weights, the change in the portfolio standardized focus gain rate of return is

$$A = \sum_j w_j M_j - \sum_i w_i M_i \qquad (10)$$

where the portfolio items before and after the change are subscripted as i and j respectively. Similarly, the change in the portfolio standardized focus loss rate of return is[6]

$$K = \sum_j w_j N_j - \sum_i w_i N_i. \qquad (11)$$

We can now bring these possible changes together in a portfolio change A/K ratio. In Figure 20 the magnitude of the A/K ratio is indicated by the slopes of the vectors emanating from the already established portfolio point P.

As the objective of the marginal portfolio change is to raise the decision maker to a higher indifference curve on his decision map it follows that the portfolio change decision criterion can be stated in terms of a critical value of the A/K ratio, or the slope of the indifference curve at the existing portfolio point. Let us refer to this critical

[6]We have designated an increase in portfolio standardized focus gain as A, the English transliteration of the initial letter of the Greek word *agathos*, meaning "good." The K derives from the Greek *kakos*, meaning "bad."

value as θ. Then for a portfolio change that involves a value of K greater than zero, the move will be desirable if A/K is greater than θ. If the contemplated portfolio change involves a K value equal to zero, the desirability condition will be satisfied provided A is positive. If, when change is contemplated the K value is negative, the desirability condition requires that the A/K ratio should be less than θ. These desirability conditions are depicted by the arrowheads in Figure 20. Portfolio change will thus be desirable if

$$\begin{aligned} &\text{for } K > 0, \quad && A/K > \theta; \\ &\text{for } K = 0, \quad && A > 0; \\ &\text{for } K < 0, \quad && A/K < \theta. \end{aligned} \tag{15}$$

The conditions summarized in the equation and inequality set (15) encompass a vast range of possible reasons for portfolio changes. But embedded in the analysis is the fact that change may occur simply because the potential surprise curve described over possible outcomes may have moved favorably in relation to one or more assets. This may occur because, among other reasons, a favorable possibility has emerged of speculative capital gain, and because of the beneficial termination of an asset holding period which resulted. Our decision theoretic structure is thus no longer locked into the stationariness of the holding period return prospects, which obscures the practical relevance of the portfolio equilibrium asset choice theory.

Economic Judgment

Our theoretical approach to the problem of decision making under uncertainty has provided adequate scope for the incorporation of the judgments that have to be made and which are made in fact in real-world financial affairs. This is a strength of the analysis. Rather than assuming away the uncertainties for what they are and where they really exist, or reducing them to certainties or certainty equivalents by stochastic reduction methods where the calculus of distributional variables cannot properly apply, the real-world decision maker's responsibility has been identified and provided with a logically robust framework of analysis for dealing with it.

Rational evaluation of alternatives compels the marshaling of relevant nondistributional variables into a coherent pattern for purposes of comparison and choice. This initial step is accomplished by the consideration of the degree of disbelief contained within the individual's outcome potential surprise function. Assumptions of continuity are not essential to the case, and comparisons of discrete possibilities might be made in appropriate cases.

Individual judgment enters also in the ranking of the relative attractiveness, or the power to focus the decision maker's attention, of combinations of potential surprise and its associated possible outcome magnitude. When a decision maker finds that each of several activity alternatives has a power to focus his attention on a suitably defined "best" and "worst" possible outcome, these different sets of "bests" and "worsts" can be brought into comparison with each other by reducing them to "standardized" equivalents. Judgments at this stage need not partake of the mathematical precision that might appear to inhere in the analysis as it has been presented. The main conclusion is that judgments involving comparisons between economic alternatives have to be made, and a quite simple and straightforward *modus operandi* for making them has now been proposed.

The decision maker's judgment enters finally in his marshaling of the preceding results in his decision map for the final isolation of choice. Here a simple ranking of alternative possibilities is called for, with the indifference curves in this final decision map reflecting the degree of uncertainty-aversion with which an individual approaches his situation and decision responsibilities.

These layers of decision responsibility, and of the scope for the exercise of judgment, return to economic analysis an appreciation of the true function of entrepreneurial management in economic affairs. This clearly is not the place to embark on a fuller discussion of the entrepreneurial function. But this much can be said: recognizing as we have the everpresent and the everpressing uniqueness of the decision moment and the decision responsibility, the temptation to abolish the decision function by replacing it with a set of mechanical rules has been abjured.

For if we mistakenly imagine that the uncertainties of the world are reducible to risk or to certainty equivalents by probability reduction methods, and if we imagine that the uniqueness of economic time can be abolished by capturing its import in a once-and-for-all risk-return preference ordering or utility function, the abolition of decision choice and decision responsibility is complete. In the act of juxtaposing a certainty equivalent magnitude and a stable preference ordering, we are no longer dealing with genuine economic choice at all. Choice has in such a case been replaced by an automatic specification of an outcome by a comprehensively prespecified mechanical rule.

Choice has genuine meaning only when it is addressed to perceived alternatives in conditions of genuine uncertainty, choices between the perceptions of outcomes conjured in the mind and imagination of the decision maker. It is the recognition of the profound implications of these realities that brings a new freshness and relevance to economics as an intellectual discipline, and to the art of enterprise management and business administration.

Subject Index

Author Index

www.ingramcontent.com/pod-product-compliance
Lightning Source LLC
LaVergne TN
LVHW010648300926
849161LV00005B/1063